The Grey Islands

THE GREY ISLANDS

John Steffler

Brick Books

CANADIAN CATALOGUING IN PUBLICATION DATA

Steffler, John, 1947–
　The grey islands

Poems.
ISBN 1-894078-13-6

1. Newfoundland – Poetry. I. Title.

PS8587.T346G73   2000   C811'.54   C00-932604-9
PR9199.3.S7814G73   2000

Copyright © John Steffler, 2000

We acknowledge the support of the Canada Council for the Arts for our publishing programme. The support of the Ontario Arts Council is also gratefully acknowledged.

Cover photo is courtesy of the author and his own photograph has been taken by Susan Gillis.

Typeset in Trump. The stock is acid-free Zephyr Antique laid. Printed and bound by the Porcupine's Quill Inc.

Brick Books
431 Boler Road, Box 20081
London, Ontario, N6K 4G6

brick.books@sympatico.ca

For my father and mother

Introduction

I have just re-read *The Grey Islands*. I knew, and thought I knew well, this story of a man's self-selected (I want, almost, to say self-inflicted, the ensuing weeks are so stripped of any familiar face or comfort) journey to and isolation on a small island off the far-north coast of Newfoundland – and I have for all the years since its first publication in 1985 felt it to be one of the very few really-and-truly original works of that decade in this country. And of all of the next decade too, it's now possible to say.

Reading it again this week, front to back, not just the browsing that I've often permitted myself, I find myself moved not merely by the pristine nature of the language – this I hadn't lost touch with at all, I doubt if any reader does – but by, and to say this is to say something different, the integrity of the enterprise. And yes, I do mean both enterprises here: that of the narrator, reporting on his journey, and that of a man standing behind, farther back than, that narrator. This being John Steffler, who somehow, hard to feel sure how, must have kept his very clear eyes on almost every minute and every page of the enterprise, must have known with a lot of certainty what he wanted and needed to say and, no less important, known what he wasn't going to allow himself to get even close to saying. If you think about it, you'll know how much that last matters.

Accounts of solitary travellers, wanderers, men or women testing themselves against Nature, against desert or floe or mountain, abound. Some of these glow against whatever their background is and outlast their generation. Many more, though, many many more, in my reading-experience, sooner or later fail to remember where they are, forget what images their pages and their narrating sensibilities will always, if they are truthful, stay very close to, and begin to find themselves interesting in ways that sure enough are a real part of their wider lives, but that have very little – nothing, to be blunt – to do with the purity of what they tell us they're engaged in. Easy enough to name names here, but since it's easy why bother. I think I've said what I needed to say.

Steffler and his narrator do what each of them separately set out to do. They head off into an almost archaic place with its own completely convincing palette of acts and colours and sounds. They inhabit this place for the entire length of their stay without striking a single faux-noble attitude or uttering the kind of familiarly plangent epitaph for the rest of us that a reader, this one anyway, feels such limitless gratitude for the absence of. And all of this in a text that is so rifted with the 'ore,' as Keats said, of real poetry that I hours ago gave up the thought of proving this through quotations. It's very, very easy to find.

Don Coles

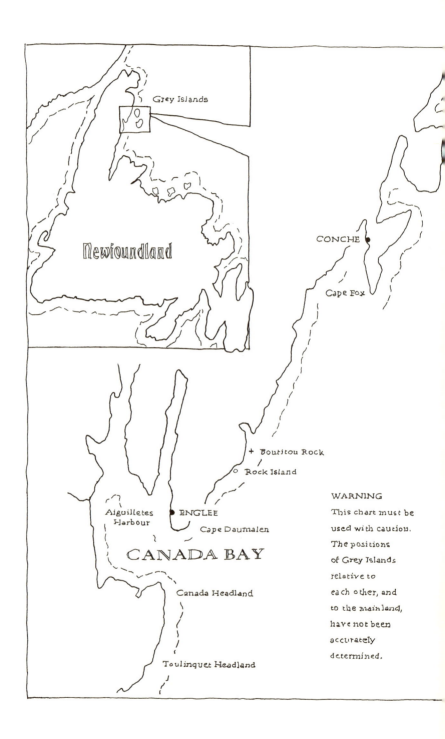

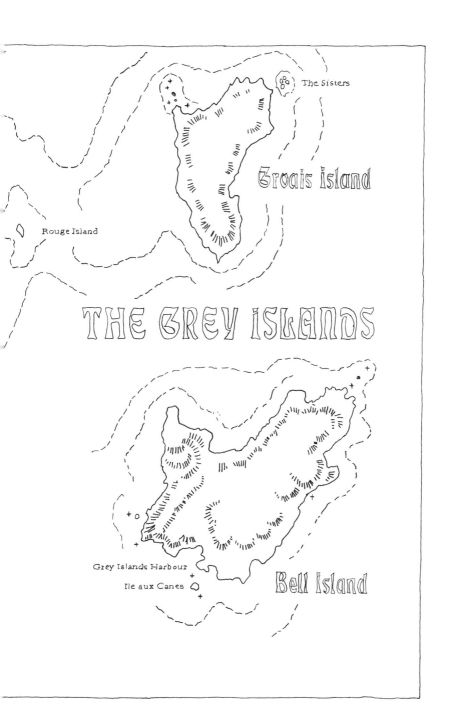

•

The island floating ahead of me like a moon, tugging me forward. Whatever it has in store.

Leonard Quinton saying, 'the voices in those old homes.' And there it was, pulling and me already going its way. An island of voices and ghosts. But ghosts and voices are everywhere. Even along the road. Flashing by. Stop and let them speak.

A way to corner myself is what I want. Some blunt place I can't go beyond. Where excuses stop.

Leonard Quinton

The 1920s, that was the big time on the Grey Islands. There were five thousand people out there in the summers then and big fishing premises in Grey Islands Harbour, where the houses still stand, and in French Cove and McGraths Cove.

In stormy weather the harbour would fill with ships, all the schooners in off the banks and down from the island's coves, which are just dents in the cliffs mostly, not places you'd choose to ride out a storm. And they'd gather in Grey Islands Harbour by the hundreds. Masts like a forest filling the bay.

Now there's nothing out there at all, just a herd of caribou.

CENSUS OF NEWFOUNDLAND: 1921

Locality: Groais Islands

Population	123
Those born in Newfoundland	122
Those born elsewhere	1
Persons under 15 years	51
Persons 15 to 30 years	32
Persons 30 to 50 years	29
Persons 50 to 80 years	11
Persons over 80 years	0
Married persons, male	24
Married persons, female	23
Roman Catholic	122
Church of England	1
Paupers	0
Crippled or disabled	0
Crazy or lunatic	0
Idiotic or silly	0
Orphans under 15	1
Males engaged in catching and curing fish	35
Females engaged in curing fish	20
Farmers	0
Clergymen	0
Doctors	0
Merchants and traders	0
Teachers	1
Persons otherwise employed	0

1

•
driving all day. mist and rain. the highway
deserted. miles of bunchbacked spruce. grey sea
butting the rock.

along the mud road to Roddickton. dark backwoods
feeling. bush on all sides. gravel pits. old
machines along the way.

hardly a soul.

- This man waiting there! The thing I can't get out of my mind. The last thing Leonard mentioned. Practically tossed it in the window as I drove off, like it hardly mattered at all. *A madman is living alone out there.* The one inhabitant left. Holding out in the ruined town. Holding the whole island in his head. Thinking it into reality, every stick, every bird. And god knows what else. What will he do when I step into his thoughts?

- Horses up ahead, foals and mothers, a whole shaggy herd scattering off the road to watch me pass. Eyes full of casual mockery. A trail of turds right down the centre line.

- Karen gone. Peter and Anna gone. House closed up. The fact hitting me more and more real. I won't be seeing them all summer long. And I feel stupid all by myself, want to turn back, recall, revise everything. But the road's too narrow to turn around and the few side trails go by so fast I miss every one of them.

-

Cow Head. The sign briefly points, a small road branching, winding among dunes and I want to follow it, imagining long-legged piers, sand spits trailing houses into the sea, but the pavement unrolls smoothly pulling me north, motion itself a tunnel, a spell, and I miss the turn, my chance of seeing Cow Head the way so many chances beckon flickering past, the streams, the little graveyards fenced with sticks, and high on a gravel beach a man spreading nets, his single boat perched on a spruce pole ramp and I want to talk to him, follow into his words, find him alone at dawn launching himself off the earth's edge, I could do it, stop *here,* let this be the spot it starts, rock, sea opening to whatever they really hold, but I don't, he's gone and I'm still zooming on, the car packed with bedding boots maps and the camera ready for use, I take the hills and valleys in a swoop as though the force it took to tear me away from home has not yet spent itself, and I just grip the wheel and go.

-

The brutal mechanics of having a wish come true.

- Four years and I'm still like a tourist here. I haven't even left the motel.

- The first job they gave me, their new town planner straight from U of T, when they'd driven me round the place, thriving Milliken Harbour, and we sat in the 'conference room,' myself and the councilmen – two contractors, the fish-plant manager, and the man with the liquor commission franchise – and I asked were there any areas that needed immediate attention, and they all agreed the bears was a headache this time o'year, tearin the hell outa the town dump, a danger to folks goin out there, and some of them roamin right into town, everyone phonin worried complainin night and day, and you couldn't stop the young fellers goin out for a lark and gettin the bears drunk and tryin to ride on their backs, and one day somebody'd get killed and sure as hell the council'd be to blame. They wanted to talk about cheap fencing and scarecrows and machines that go bang every thirty seconds. I got them a grant and had an incinerator put in, and that's still the most popular thing I've done. Four years ago. And the rest has been mostly road signs and litter barrels and organizing the odd parade.

Town planner. Town joe-boy is what I've been. But whose fault is that? I'd find lots to do if this place meant anything to me. Or if the people wanted to change a thing. And I'm dying bit by bit, shrinking, drying up along with my dreams of the New Jerusalem, the four-gated golden city with market squares and green belts and pedestrian streets and old buildings restored and tourist money pouring in. I laugh at that now, an old pain I screw myself with, and every once in awhile (like every day) it hits me I've got to get out of here to save what's left of me, and I keep up with the trade magazines and write to people I used to know, but there's nothing going, there isn't a job from here to B.C. And I think then how lucky I am, Bill driving cab in Toronto for Christ sake and David in some office block in Ottawa, and I figure I'll sit tight till something turns up, at least it's a good place to raise kids. That's one lie that's easy to swallow. There's lots of fresh air and there isn't much crime and the people are friendly is what I always say, the people are wonderful. And we head for the mainland every chance we get, Karen dying for Yonge and Bloor, Kensington Market, Spadina Avenue. And I'm dying for it too. We get there and drag ourselves over the sidewalks and I hate the place. Two weeks every year. We're like ghosts looking for something we've lost. The city changes in four years, people move, we don't have a home. And we change too. We fade slowly. Into ghosts.

•
always the fear I'll
somehow run amok

the stories:
they went to get him at the summer's end
the cabin open
cold porridge on the stove
never a trace of him

how he went mad and jumped from a cliff
was abducted by spirits
fell down a pirate treasure shaft and
walked into Shangri-La.
burned his clothes and hid in the trees
until everyone sailed away

•

All that tension the past month. Days gone by in a blur. The trouble with breaking attachments, ending routines.

The council boys cautiously nodding, 'Sure. OK. A leave of absence if you want.' Patey of course: 'Are ya sure we shouldn't be lookin for a new town planner?' And I tell them again I'll let them know in September, I just need time off. And their eyes shift away. But they're good enough to wish me luck.

With Karen it's a different thing. She knows why I'm doing this, approves even, sees signs of life in my decision. And summer in Ontario is a dream for her, the stores and films, days at the lake. And in a way she's just as glad to go without me, my restlessness a bother to her when we're there. But still. A whole summer apart. Both of us wondering is this how the end begins? And she's annoyed because it's my initiative, and she's left to react, do what she has to because of me. Stuck with the kids. While I'm off indulging in masculine idleness, chasing a selfish whim. As soon as I mentioned it she started guarding herself, taking charge of her fatherless brood like I was just visiting. Tough, going back to her family alone though. All of them so alert to the smell of divorce. Quick with contingency plans, personal strategies. They'll take her into their arms, drooling condolences, and she'll have to say over and over, 'It's not like that!' Hating my guts.

-

This damn guy gets in the way of everything!

Just before setting out, my mind full of that pure island – me rising strong and clear-edged, carving my habits out of the uncut days – I called on Leonard Quinton to say goodbye. It was then, remembering one last bit of advice, he said, 'Oh. There might be a man still out on the island. Carm Denny's his name. But don't let him worry you. He's sure to be more afraid of you than you are of him. He'll run and hide if you try to call on him.'

And I heard in a daze about Carm Denny's struggles with little folk, listening devices, fire. His charms and offerings and armaments. His notions and visions. And visions! I'm getting visions too! Visions of me trying to meditate on the tide knowing this froth-jawed fighter of devils and Martians is scanning my every move through the sights of a gun. Visions of two gaunt men stalking one another boulder by boulder over the island hills.

Visions! Visions!

- I'm going not for the island only now, the space and solitude. But to meet this man who's spent his life out there.

Not just playing around.

One look and I'll see what I'd become completely alone.

- Parsons Pond. Low buildings. Take-outs, confectioneries hiked up on stilts next to the shoulder. Girls on the highway three abreast, eating French fries. Two-hundred pounders. Sausaged into their jeans. I wave and give them a wide berth. People always strolling right on the pavement here. Bored and playing chicken with the passing cars. Hunting bold proposals, long rides. And why should cars have the only pavement to themselves? All the rest of the place puddles, potholes and broken rock. And the road is where people have always walked. A guy in a car no more important than someone in rubber boots. I like this. Blocking the highway while you chat with a few friends.

•
hunting country.
hills and ponds poker-faced,
guarded.

close to the road, small
quick-built homes, pickups, skidoos
parked among trees. people
live light
able to strike fast at

things that are passing by:
animals, birds, fish, work,
money in any form.

•
down the last hill and
it's Englee.
good junky bustle.
rocks and houses tossed together. gulls
and rigging. boats docked among roofs it looks.
planks crossing ditches to candy shacks. Hostess
Coke Rothmans signs trailing down their
fronts like medals, honorary
membership in that world.

I park, spattered pickups all around,
and walk the muddy harbour lane.
stages, wharves, woodpiles, sheds
patched propped tilting grey clamber over the water.
sunk cars waving kelp, boats rotting keel up,
chickens, nets, rusting drums.

houses back up tight to the cliff.

every window curtain shifts.
pale hands, faces rise
from crocheted shadows.

kids walk by say hello. turn. walk by again. hello.
pass again for another look.

one guy in back of his pickets chopping wood.
I say hello. he bends, his hands in the chips,
watches me under his arm.

- At the airport though in that last white minute under the lights, it was good, it was stronger than ever between us. No trace of desertion or revenge. That date in September, that goal, all of us coming home, the strongest thing in our lives. The frame for everything else.

Lifting Peter and Anna, feeling their slender arms was the hardest thing, knowing I'll find them older and grown when I touch them again. To miss so much of their lives.

•
he's out there the kids say pointing.
a little hut. the far end of a loose beaver dam.
Nels's stage.
must be so familiar to him and his family
they don't even see it anymore,
run, scramble sure-footed over the holes
and wobbles.

to me it's a jungle.
trip-vines, man-traps, where do you put your feet
for godsake, gaps, loose sticks teeter-totter,
water right under you.
hello!
I poke my head in the low door, rafters
dangling every kind of gaff and rusty implement.
an old man at the splitting table.
two boys perch watching him sharpen
squid jiggers with a file.

he shakes my hand, cautious,
feeling what kind of man.
traveller. landsman.
(salesman? missionary? taxman? crook?)
I want to get to the island I tell him,
hear he takes people out.

he spits. goes back to filing.
it spiles a day, he warns.

then flings out what it'll cost.
if we can go on the water.

I wait.

am I with the government?
no no! I'm (what'll I call myself?)

I just want to spend some time out there.
fish for trout.

he cuts his price in half.

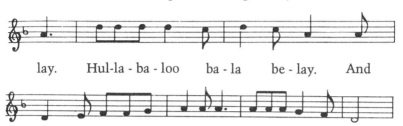

Me mo-ther kept a board-ing house, Hul-la-ba-loo be-lay. Hul-la-ba-loo ba-la be-lay. And all the boarders was out to sea, Hul-la-ba-loo be-lay.

Of course there's room!
There's always room.
Albert's in Walter's room and Lonz's comin back,
but Jewelleen's in Roddickton.
You can have her bed for a night.

•
squeezed under the roof
Jewelleen's room's just big enough for a bed
and a *real* moviestar vanity table
complete with lightbulb-studded mirror,
dangling lockets and scarves,
a dozen quart bottles of red perfume.

the walls, even the ceiling bag down with
magazine photos of famous stars,
cute boys, couples holding hands in the daisies,
guys screaming, electrocuted by guitars.
I move the powder-blue portable record player
and put down my pack, the window
grips into the harbour's
primitive works
the matted hills, the sea heaped up
grey.

•

End of the day-shift one guy comes in hearty and joking, bangs down his lunch pail rolling his sleeves. A red-haired fellow drifts in from a bar. I answer their questions, talk of the island, the fishing. They pick up from yesterday or the day before, laughing about how drunk Clifford Burton had got. Left him wrapped in a cod trap back of his own boat.

Suppertime. Two more men pad down the stairs, rumpled and blinking. Nod shyly. Night-shift workers or invalids. Hard to tell. We all sit.

Tea bag, cup of hot water by every plate. Stuffed squids on a platter. Potatoes. Half the kids squeeze onto a bench down one side, nudging, whispering. Others eat in the kitchen.

Mrs Brake at the head of the table. Says grace.

'Does ya mind the tails?' she calls. I stop, mouth full, look at my plate. Tiny dirigibles. Noses sewn shut. Tail fins in place at the back.

'No,' I say, stab, bite another, 'tail meat's the same as the rest.' All the kids giggle, writhe, choke, go red in the face.

'Oh, *I* can't eat 'em,' she says. 'I doesn't know why, just never could fancy 'em.' She purses her lips, arches her pinkies, plucks the flukes off another squid.

The daughters all do like Mom. Line the little brown tails up on the edge of their plates.

•

After supper the daughters all fight, do dishes, take turns slamming the bathroom door.

I stand in the empty parlour. Ashtray-carpet smell. Bride-dolls veiled in dust on the TV. Last Supper tapestry, silver and navy blue. One wall covered in family photographs: Christmas, Mom, all 10 or 20 kids lined up in their Sunday best, more of Mom. No sign of a father anywhere. A bounder? Runaway? Wouldn't disgrace the wall with his face?

Maybe a different father for every one.

Easy now. Might be a virtuous lady joined to an unphotogenic man. Badly disfigured. Kept in the attic. Tale of bitter suffering there.

Maybe a Sufi. Scared of losing his soul.

Or he's the only one who can use a camera. Shutter-bug mariner. Comes ashore. Click click. Night with the wife. Next day back on the bounding main. Obvious answer.

•

In Englee they tell me Uncle Carm's not out there this year. Got pretty strange and the RCMP took him off late last fall. He's in St. John's now. In the mental.

The relief when I hear this! The future, the island, the whole summer handed back to me. Clear and wide. It all seems easy now.

An island's so much simpler than another man.

- Nels and his wife and half a dozen or so of his kids are loading empty barrels into a boat. 'Goin squiddin,' Nels says.

I ask if there's room for me.

'Y'ever done it before?'

'Nope.'

'It's terrible dirty work,' he warns, his eyes bright with glee.

I tell him that's okay, and he sends his youngest boy to find me a pair of rubber trousers.

I step into them, pull the braces up and grab a barrel to take aboard.

They do me the favour of letting me try to help.

Later Nels moves the barrel to where it was meant to be.

●
evening water. white.
soft as a bird.
we putt-putt-putt past headlands grey as clouds,
rolling our milky wake.

deep in the hills
a thin bay.
boats Nels knows, five,
six families already there, rocking,
drifting, knocking together
over the swarming squid. like a
village picnic, everyone beckons
calling,
        and we drop anchor, drift
in with the rest.
sweet sea smells stirring the warm air.

That's where I was born, Nels says, pointing.
head of the bay: a beach-side meadow, bright
fireweed on the smoky slope.

not a building in sight.

●
grey silk we sway on

salt-grey smells

sky and hills shedding a powder-grey glow
even the boat's thick paint glows china white
and our faces, peach, copper, cream-yellow
round, our faces
glow in the cotton air like lamps

•
they all save one last squirt
till they're clear of the water,
black splats straight in the air,
up your sleeve, into your eye.

we sit tossing our jiggers,
ducking, chuckling, piling up squids
easy as pie.

'Take a chunk outa ya big as a dime,'
Nels says, shaking one down that's
braided around his arm.

'Fall in there and they'd drown ya,
drag ya down.'

dark in the water long forms shoot crisscross
like limbs of a sunken forest. strange.
not the same things we're pulling in,
stringy legs, flabby pouches.

coming up they ink wildly, puff like
parachutes. trying to put on the brakes.

dying they make small sunsets
with their bodies. glow blood-orange, freckle
like trout, huff, sigh. drain iridescent
green. lemon. white.

'Dry 'em on a line,' Nels says. 'Wintertime,
put 'em in a toaster same as a slice a bread.
Sure! Better'n potato chips!'

• to Nels and his family,
going to live alone on an island is madness,
terrifying to contemplate.

I can see a shrinking point in their eyes
when they ask me: 'Won't ya get lonely out there?'
they know these islands, stories of people
lost, stranded, gone mad.
I answer, 'No.'
and then, 'At least I don't *think* I will.'
since it's a tricky question with me too
and as much as I'd like to put them at ease,
show that I'm no harebrained mainlander
off to blithely feed himself to the sea,
I don't want to boast. because
I don't know what the night and the island spirits
will do to me.
and more than anything else
I'm afraid of pride.

- back to a station on their journey.
things left behind. the air
still ringing where they were.
my journey too.
tracing the same road two ways.

• Coming back late, I figure most of them sleeping now. Just slip up the stairs and to bed. But down the dark street the Brakes' looks like an old-fashioned radio going full blast. Every window lit. Door open. Shouting and crying clear five houses away. Oh Christ.

Glass crunches on the front steps. I poke my head in the parlour, furnace of bedlam, someone stretched on the sofa, face under a towel. The red-haired guy standing swinging his head like a bull, Mrs Brake pushing him shrieking, 'Go Jim, git! Go to sleep! You know you'll be sorry tomorrow!' 'Sorry! Pfaw! Feel good,' Jim slurs. 'Bash his fuckin face in. Momma's suck.'

The man on the sofa lifts his towel, thin face bloody, singing, 'You're the chicken, you're the chicken, fraid a work, fraid a boats, big man drunko, big man drunk!' Quick covers his face again. Jim wheels, pounds what's under the towel, a voice rising muffled, broken by thuds: 'Go on! *ump* Kill me! *ump* Big bully!' Mrs Brake knots one hand in the back of Jim's hair, the other clawing his ear his collar, trying to drag him away. I step in, get hold of his shirt, haul him down on his butt.

'Who's this?' he says slowly, staring, eyes crossing. 'Fuckin mainlander.... Think you own the fuckin world.... *Holiday*.... Go to fuckin Disneyland.' Mrs Brake cuts in clutching her chest, 'Okay mister, you run along now, have a nice sleep, this is nothin here.' But Jim's up coming at me, and Mrs Brake shrill as a siren grabs a softball trophy off the TV, hits him once from behind. Nothing. She rears back, swings again, his eyes jolt white, jaws working froth, he goes to his knees, pitches face down on the floor.

'There,' she says, setting the trophy back on the TV.

•

Seeing us turn, the guy on the couch hides a frail gloat and starts moaning, rolling side to side. Mrs Brake strokes his hair, dabs his face like a tray of raw sausages. 'There, there. ... Oh Jim gits him all riled up! He won't sleep again tonight now see, and he's not well, he's only got the one kidney and that's mine, the one I give him, and I only got one lung, didn't know that did ya mister, I'm not strong, and he gits infections so easy, and he bleeds and he bleeds and he don't heal. Doctor says he got no heemagoblins in him. But Jim there gits to drinkin and teasin him, and this one here won't keep still like I tells him. 'Let'm talk,' I says, 'let'm be. He aint hisself when he's drunk.' Oh gits right ugly, right *evil* he does.'

Others looking in at the door. Girls in dressing gowns, whispering.

'But let'm talk like I says and he'll drink hisself to sleep and not remember a thing in the mornin. Finest sort in the world Jim is when he's sober. Quietest kind. But he's got a weakness sir. Spends every cent of money he gits on drink. Can't keep a job. Can't do a tap of work. And this one nags him about it. This one'd *like* to work if he could. Saves every cent of money he ever got. Even bought a *car*.'

The sound of a water tap. A cupboard door bangs in the kitchen. Mrs Brake calls, 'Cindy! Put the kettle on!'

'Thanks for your help,' she tells me, weary, lying back in a chair. 'You go to bed now mister, have a nice sleep.'

•
I shut my door. *Nice sleep!* Where the hell am I? What am I doing here? Pack's been moved. Done up a different way. I dig in fast.

Wallet's not where I left it.

Find it, flip it open, counting. Forty bucks short. Bugger! *Bugger!* Own fault leaving it here. Probably paid for Jim's night on the town. Criminal negligence leaving money near *that* guy.

Christ! Love to see Jewelleen's posture. Grew up sleeping in this! Butt hanging down to the floor, feet sticking up six inches in front of your face.

Her smell in the sheets. Perfume and hair.

Feel strangely close to that absent woman. jammed into her body's mould. One night in somebody else's rack. The whole place. The poor people living here. Cage of god-awful misery. Good night Elvis. Good night Ringo. Pull the lightbulb string.

Tomorrow the island I hope. Fresh space.

•
how well do you know yourself?
the various people
waiting inside.

heroes, hysterics, killers
who push to the front of the crowd
when things go wrong

•
good early sun.
last of the night clouds broken,
racing away.
the sea running high after rain

out from Englee we buck, slew in the
first of the waves, the deck
drops under me and I grab
the hatch, start
learning the dives and dodges

•
scoured sky. wind
and open miles.
all morning we climb the bright
hills cresting across our course,
pitching us up, sledding us sideways
down, wallowing, walled in water.
     quick. near us
and gone,
  slim birds flit low, banking,
twisting, skimming the closing troughs,
and I feel it,
   know it a laughing
fact: the harder your hungry eyes bite
into the world (the island cliffs pencilled
in blue haze, and *there,* Nels pointing:
whale spray!
    huge flukes kicking at the sun), the more
you spread your arms to hug it in,
the less you mind the thought of diving under,

eyes flooded. gulping dark.

2

•
cliffs
and a thin green
cover. like
dinosaurs crouching under a rug. then

through the rowdy narrows
a sunlit bay: spits, shoals and islands, white
birds lifting out of the blue. no

centre. no shadows here. no lines
leading anywhere. waves
capes scrub-tufts shift, shuffle

under the open sky.

•

Two rock paws. Between them a gravel beach, a wharf,
the cabin crouched ten feet from the shore. A white
door and a stoop facing the waves. Long grass ducking,
galloping up a hill.

A thick pitted padlock is held to the door with spikes.
Splinters and holes up and down where it's been ripped out
and hammered back. A contest. Keepers and takers. Owners
and travellers. Out here the law is the other way. The right
to shelter takes first place.

Stove, table, two metal bunks. Mattresses once used in
bayonet practice probably. Yellow linoleum nailed to the
table top, dirt deep in the cracks and gashes. Chain oil,
blood, rust, fat, scrawled in like a diary. All the guys gutting
their ducks and fish here, cleaning their guns, stripping their
engines down, hands dripping black spreading bolts and
bearings among the plates of beans.

Feathers turn and lift in the corners when you walk. Back of
the stove mush-bottomed boxes, plastic bags bloated with
rot, shrunk potatoes gone into sprouts, liquid carrots,
cabbages yellow, burst.

Men coming here at the end of their calculations and budgets
and fights and fantasies. Building into crude space. A good
time hacking and arsing out at the furthest edge. No home.
No sofas. No wives. High boots, hunting knives and booze
and not getting washed. Then, the time used up or unable to
stand it another day, laughing and boasting they run to their
boats or planes, dropping what nobody owns. And half what
they brought. Cupboard crammed with stale pancake mix,
margarine, sugar, salt. Salt for godsake! Like me everybody
brings salt. Nobody takes it away.

- Nels didn't like bringing his boat up to the wharf here. Too many rocks around. He steered with his body half out the window fussing and muttering to himself, me watching the other side ready to shout. He saw me ashore and then we shook hands and he jumped back on board. 'You're the boss here now,' he called over the diesel's racket, and he eased his boat back out.

Some of the stories he told. Amazing things.

● climbing slowly
up from the bay
the rock's sweet lichen
crackling under foot
the cabin roof a small
molten square
I spread my arms in the cool sea wind
bathe my face long
long in the inexhaustible blue

•
dark falling

across the file-grey cove
a flat spit of land

black skeleton houses. rumbling sky

•
Nels

It was late in the fall of the year. We was bringin the mail from Harbour Deep, young Michael Thoms and me, and we put into Hooping Harbour for the night on account of weather. The fishin families was gone by that time and there wasn't a soul in the place. Only the old houses back of the cove. You could just pick them out through the blowin snow. Black holes where the doors and windows used to be.

I remember it gettin dark around three o'clock that day. The fiercest kind of storm out of the nor-east, but comin down over the land there, so we was set pretty comfortable off the lee shore and tied close to the wharf.

We had the lamp lit and was boilin the kettle for tea, neither of us sayin much. We was glad to be below was all. And I was listenin to the wind, thinkin she might shift and we'd have to get the boat farther out, when all of a sudden there was a *clomp-clomp* up on the deck. And the boat tilted, and rose again. The hair on the back of my neck stood up stiff as a brush. Somebody had stepped aboard.

I looked at Michael, and my *son*, his face was white as a sheet. 'It must be a big man,' he whispers to me, 'the way she went down under his feet.'

We waited, right still in our seats, but all we could hear was the wind and the water breakin across the cove. 'Hey!' I shouted, 'Who's there?' There wasn't a sound up top. I shouted again, 'Hey! Who's out there?'

Nothin. Not a noise.

We sat for the longest time scarcely takin a breath. And then there came the sound – right faint at first – of someone touchin the hatch, someone lightly rattlin the latch, scratchin the wood with his nails, quietly, quietly. And then louder and louder. I jumped up, grabbed a guttin knife and threw the hatch back ready for anythin. Snow and cold wind come pourin over me, and a cat, an ugly grey cat jumped down on the table where we had our plates of food.

I'd never seen such an ugly animal before, like somethin dead that was up walkin around. Starved I guess it was. Left behind by some fishermen at the season's end. Its hair matted flat, more like felt than fur, and its head too big for it – round as a ball – with its yellow eyes poppin out. But the way it moved, that was the worst thing about it. Right stiff it was, and awkward, like there was machinery under its hide instead of bones.

And yet it wasn't slow. I found *that* when I tried to grab it. Stiff as rusty shears, but steady b'y, and desperate not to get caught. I went after it under the table, back of the stove, over the bunks, and finally cornered it on some rope up in the bow of the boat. It didn't scratch or hiss or nothin when I picked it up. It just went on movin its legs like it was wound up with a key. And the strange thing was it didn't feel skinny at all. It felt thick and heavy like it was made of wood inside.

And it wasn't warm. But cold. Cold as mud.

It made me right sick to my stomach, that thing. just the feel of it. I hove it overboard the minute I got my head clear of the hatch.

We cast off then and anchored about fifty feet out. Neither of us slept a wink that night.

• last night a dream

a worldly young woman walking
beside me, her hand down
my trousers holding my cock
and smiling

liking me.

I took this to be a good omen

that I'll be blessed with the chance
to do some good work.

•

Went fishing first thing this morning. As soon as I left the cabin the flashes of happiness started. The new light. The chest-deep grass you wade through along the path. Low intricate shrubs – birds flitting ahead every step – each feature so strong. So sharp in the new air.

Down in the salt meadow a brook winds out. Hills rising above, rugged, lush in the early sun. The absolute solitude. Sound of distant surf. Short grass underfoot, thick, level as lawn.

Walked up the brook through alder thicket to a pool below falls – the water peat-black and sleek – and there quickly caught two trout – one good-sized one.

I cleaned the fish and kept them cool, then climbed up to the bare plateau on top of the island. The air was not just clear, but washed, polished, an active medium able to intensify each object, speed and refine the movement of light.

Birds glided past in perfectly smooth steady lines as though drawn across the sky by some precision instrument. They appeared to exert no effort, to be absent from themselves – their wings clean-cut, pointed, slim.

In mid-afternoon I came down to the cabin tired and very hungry. Made a meal of fried potatoes and trout sprinkled with lemon juice – a good idea to bring the lemons along. I ate sprawled in the open door looking out at the white surf and the blue bay. The trout's flesh was reddish orange and sweet.

●
I thought I was headed for silence
but this island blares and bustles
as hard as any town

the sea slops and thumps
gurgles and knocks
suddenly loud
    (so close I turn expecting some
      person or creature climbing the bank)
suddenly muffled
steered away by the wind rustling
the grass, whispering up the wall

and the gulls
their single distant cries piercing
the shore's roar
their spiral bickering, jeers,
griefs, alarms
sharpen the air: salt
made audible.

even a bumble bee
touring slowly in at the door
and out
can make the cabin hum like a guitar

-

One of the last things Nels talked about. An hour out from Englee and he stared at me for a while, and then over the engine's noise he said, 'Ya don't mind bein alone I guess?'

'No,' I said, 'it's what I want.'

'Ya don't see things then like some folks. Ghosts and that.'

'No,' I said. 'Not so far.' And we laughed and he started to tell me what some of the old-timers used to see out here. Fairies and hags and a man the priest turned into a goat. But above all Mother Burke.

'She was the real island ghost,' he said, 'the regular one. There was three men went huntin ptarmigan down to the north island there this one time and when they was set to come home and was pushin off from shore they seen the bow of their boat go down just like someone had climbed aboard of her. The boat rode low in the water all the way back and when they got into Rocky Bay and pulled alongside their wharf, their boat tipped a bit and went up again, the way she would if someone had jumped ashore. Well, after that people kept meetin up with an old woman nobody'd ever seen before. Mother Burke they called her, and they'd see her around the harbour and in on the hills daytime or nighttime any time of the year. She was always in black with a bonnet on and a shawl or apron affair that she'd pull up over her face if ya got too close to her. They said that seein her brought bad luck, and they'd blame things on her like sickness and accidents and things they'd lost. One time when the priest was out they asked him to send her away, and he said some prayers and banished her so they said, back to the northern island, and where she landed she turned into rock in a place they call The Sisters. I know people in Conche though claims they still see her out here when they come pickin bakeapples.'

'Did you ever see her yourself?' I asked.

He looked at me for a second or two, his eyes half guarding some nakedness.

'Yes b'y, I did. One time just back of where I'm takin ya.'

•

For the past two days a longliner has been anchored out in the bay. A cloud of gulls twisting over it shows when the men are gutting their catch. After dark they run a generator and have a light on deck. The sound of the generator stops and the light goes out at about 9:30 or 10:00.

Every once in a while during the day I hear the sudden whine of their speedboat or the deeper beat of their skiff's engine, and I can't help myself: I go to the window or drop what I'm doing to look their way, thinking they might be coming here. But they never are. They zip up the bay somewhere else or out into open water.

When I first got here, I was afraid I'd never be left alone, that having the island's only wharf out front and a spring up behind would mean I'd be on the main track of everyone passing through this part of the world, and that there'd always be people camped around or wanting to share the cabin. But since the first day, I haven't seen a soul.

It's as though everyone cleared out or pulled back the minute I arrived. Whether they did this out of considerateness or shyness or hostility is hard to tell.

• the fisherman's work
frightens me.

dawn. alone
into the ice-bit wind
the featureless waves.

water. sky.
bottomless depths
on all sides.
nothing to hold to.
nothing warm.

• black spongy paths,
caribou trails, cut
deep in the wiry scrub,
wander up on the island's plateau,
fade on the rock outcrops

pick up again in the brush,
drop, skirting bogs,
fan into squishy hoof-holes
black soup
stranding you hopping tussock to tussock

then gather again with the rising ground,
thin tracks cleaving mounded moss,
juniper, blueberries, crowberries, heath,
knee-high billions of matted micro-leaves
sharp in blue light tiny fruit trembling

• by the trail
large flat-topped mushrooms
moist pearly gills on show over the bracken
'Good to eat?' I wonder
breaking one off, sniff
dank essence of earth
peer close
white flesh riddled with quick
slender grubs
I crush its cool cushiony chunks
in my fists
mashing it well through my knuckles
to know it
      its magic hits in a flash: I am
you Peter

four years old
always
this close to the world

- The unfamiliarity of the sounds of the sea combined with the fact that I'm alone here and always half expecting someone to come to the cabin makes me uneasy at night and keeps me from sleeping. An apartment above a busy street would be no worse. I expected the sea to lull me, not keep me awake.

I hear the sound in too much detail. Whole groups and tiers and ranges of sound within and behind the obvious slap and slosh, wash, thump, gurgle and slurp. I hear knocks and hisses and crackles. At times last night it sounded as though the cabin was being hit by a stream of tiny weightless particles – powdered sand in the wind or pellets of snow. I thought it could almost be the sound of fire starting, and got out of bed to look around.

• on the line
where three of the world's walls meet
where the sky is deaf and the water
and land come crashing in rubble
the sandpiper
on legs no thicker than stems of grass

skitters after the surf
leaping aside when a breaker falls,
nervous
but perfectly focused into his work
soundlessly
weightlessly darting his needle beak
quick and busy

as though the rest of the world
did not exist

•
looking south
the Horse Islands floating in blue haze
I stand on rocks scratched
and etched over by ice and wind

littered with glittering silicate chips

patched and padded with small-leaved plants
crabbed things
dry. snaking.
wadded together in knots and tuffets
black wiry hair
white crumbling lumps
claws. crisp bristling spines

everything half bone
half powdered rock

• *Nels*

There was my great-uncle Aaron Shale, one of the biggest fish-killers on the coast and a right hard man. The way a lot of 'em used to be.

He'd be out with his boy Clement – that woulda been my Uncle Clement – they'd be fishin with handlines together, and he expected the boy to jig just as many fish as he did, and as big too. He'd take a thick stick out in the boat with him, and if *he* jigged a fish and the boy didn't he'd give the boy a wallop with the stick. And not lightly neither I can tell ya. Or if *he* jigged a big fish and the boy only come up with a small one, he'd hit him for that. Oh yes sir! Catchin big fish was the sorta thing ya could do if ya had a mind to, accordin to Aaron Shale.

And by and by the boy learned, too. For a time there he could jig fish right alongside his old man.

- Under everything I'm often vaguely anxious, uneasy in the middle of my actions here. So many things strange to me. The tide for example. It constantly changes the terrain in the low shoreland east of the cabin, and I'm always a bit afraid of getting stranded there.

Paths appear and become submerged. Little knolls that I cross on foot at one time of the day and fix in my memory as landmarks, at another time of the day have turned to islands.

At low tide the sea is bordered by natural meadows. The incoming tide slides up into these grassy fields – a beautiful lush sight – but tricky as far as walking is concerned. It's often impossible to know before stepping forward into the tall grass whether my foot will find solid earth or water below the leaves – and if there is water, how deep it will be.

•
in this space and solitude
time works differently

details, things nearby
have hypnotic power

out in the tide-plain are
starfish, anemones, quick rock crab

hours pass without you noticing

when you lift your eyes
the landscape has changed.
the sea, once far away
is all around.
busy. impersonal.

paths have vanished.

the shore has wandered inland like a herd of caribou.

• when the rain comes and a cold wind
with it, it takes me by surprise:
no wood in the cabin. nothing to burn. but
I should have thought of this!
sunshine being the exception here.

I crouch shivering in front of the rusty
stove, trying the doors and vents,
not even sure if it's safe to use.

along the landwash some scattered
sticks, not too deeply soaked,
I split them, get them to burn
and then the real work starts:

braced against rain, I hack
at slippery boards all morning,
jump on them, break them
over my knee, the textbook
tenderfoot – foresight! foresight! –
scrambling now to save myself,
and hearing Nels's voice:

'When the wood's dry, *that's*
when ya cut it 'n stack it.
Not when it's soakin wet!'

'Good weather, plan for rain.
Gotta know what y're about b'y!'

arm-load by arm-load I stack my
soggy splits around the stove,
in the oven, up the wall,
keeping a careful relay:

burning wood. to dry wood.
to burn.

burning wood. to dry wood.
to burn.

•

Nels

From the month of June to the month of October, Aaron Shale never took his oilskins off. He never shifted out of 'em night or day for the whole fishin season. He was that hard at it. At eleven or twelve at night he'd come up from his boats and stores, lie down just like he was, and get up again at three in the mornin to pull his traps.

Nothin got in *his* way, my son.

And he *drove* his family, and them he had hired on, drove 'em just like he drove hisself. Never a minute's rest as long as the fish was runnin. He wouldn't so much as allow 'em to *speak* unless it had to do with the fish or the traps or what they needed to do. And he never opened his mouth hisself except to give orders, never even spoke to his wife for weeks on end. He'd come in dinner-time – and his food had to be ready, ready and waitin; she'd watch till he left the wharf, and get it all laid out hot before he opened the door – he'd walk across to his chair, sit down, eat, and walk out again without sayin a word, without even lookin at her while she stood there beside the stove.

The year his boy Clement died, the fish was some thick. They was bringin in three, four skiff-loads a day. And Aaron wouldn't take the time to put his son in the ground. He ordered the others to salt the boy, just like a fish, and he kept him like that out on his stage till the end of the season. Then they buried him. When the fish was done.

• holed up here
with five boxes of food
I'm in a constant race with bacteria
to see who can eat the most of it
first

I hunch over the table
munching and glowering.
millions of tiny eyes in the cheese and bread
glower back

my stomach tells me *(urp)*
they've just about won

if I don't give in soon
they'll be having me for dessert

• Night on the island is full of power. In the dark the land and sea are released from the spell of logic and industry the sun's light places upon them. The water, the trees and hills rise up. They roam and assume what shapes they wish.

At one point last night I stepped out of the cabin and was startled by the gigantic glaring presence of the moon, its reflection reaching in a broad flashing path down the sea, like a river of cold light falling straight to the cabin door. I had never seen the moon so large or so white, and its light seemed too sharp, too keen and alert: as if grinning – not hungrily exactly – but with knowing, exultant power, like some great animal.

It moved briskly, this creature of light, rippling its body with easy energy. And I stood swallowed up, gazing into it. But I could not bear it for long. It was too massive and too cold to confront alone. In a rush I turned back to the cabin and opened the door: the relief! the lantern throwing its cone of warm light over the table, my book, the woodstove crackling contentedly.

• having no shovel and
no knife long enough
I prowl the slippery wreckage
of one old house
find a leg from a vanished stove

and wade far out on the tide flats
my raincoat hood screening all but the
squashing kelp
the barnacled stones crackling under foot.

alone in drizzle, I stop.
sniff raw salt.
the low sea before me broad as the edge of the world.
behind: black rubble shore. half
hidden in mist.
a few gulls sliding slowly across.

I hum
warm in the pleasure of hunting.
eyes on the bubbling sand.
dig fast. lever the heavy iron

but only bring them up broken.
fat clams all gone to rags.
a stupid waste.
I throw the stove leg away and
hunch. dig like an animal
ramming sand under my nails
spade my fingers around the plump shells.
strain.
drag the muscular buggers up
their white flesh still bulging
leaking juice

• all day at the cabin

wind thundering
banging bits of the roof
rocking the walls

I feed the fire
move from window to window
watching the herded waves
the long lunging grass

CENSUS OF NEWFOUNDLAND: 1985

Locality: Grey Islands

Population 1
Those born in Newfoundland 0
Those born elsewhere 1

Persons under 15 years 0
Persons 15 to 30 years 0
Persons 30 to 50 years 1
Persons 50 to 80 years 0
Persons over 80 years 0

Married persons, male 1
Married persons, female 0

Roman Catholic 0
Church of England 0

Paupers 0
Crippled or disabled 0
Crazy or lunatic 1
Idiotic or silly 0
Orphans under 15 0

Males engaged in catching and curing fish 0
Females engaged in curing fish 0
Farmers 0
Clergymen 0
Doctors 0
Merchants and traders 0
Teachers 0
Persons otherwise employed 1

•
on the bunk, behind the stove,
every bowl and pan catching
drips, I make my rounds as if
tapping a sugar bush, empty
them all in a pail and open the door
to pitch it – rain gusting in –
I stop. seeing the cabin's afloat
in a giant pool. mountain runoff
pouring under the back wall
gurgling out at the steps. I close
the door hearing my father's voice
his solid Ontario disbelief:
'They built it in the middle of a
bog for cats' sake! And the roof!
Man-oh-man.' (in real grief)
'The flashing's on *top* of the shingles!
All the rain goes *inside!*'

I stand listening like a boy
embarrassed
ashamed to have any connection
with such a place

having no excuse that would convince *him*
no practical explanation why
people here set so little store
in staying high and dry.

• 4th day of hurricane. (3? No, 4 for sure.) Time gone to mush cooped in here nursing a fire. Hum, talk a lot, bake biscuits, wash myself, socks, towels, keep plenty of water hot, staggering out to the spring, buckets whirling my arms like a carnival ride.

Sat most of today at the table. Dusk from the time I got up. The drips, the walls jumping forward. Feel myself getting like the potatoes, soft, sprouty. Even my head changing shape. Wind wearing me down. Don't fight it I tell myself. Go with it. Join it. It'll get tired by and by.

Night again. Hissing lamp. Windows black as obsidian. Rattling sleet. *Eat* I'm telling my body. Fuel for the night. But it gazes down like an eagle perched in a cage. Jellied chicken and carrots. Cold on a plate. My body looks away.

The radio. Batteries weak. Tipping it up and down, I get the marine weather, listen close, expecting emergency bulletins, ships sunk, men lost at sea. The guy's prim voice patters on about moderate southerly winds. No word of a northeast hurricane. Where the hell is he? Broadcast booth in the heart of a bomb shelter?

I pace around blocked, bottled, can't ask, can't reach out, summons, contact, move. Can't budge. Can't change a thing.

The cabin cartwheels into the night. Black end-of-the-world ocean. Miles and miles. Not a light. Not a man.

•
Ontario.
flat now under the August sun.
Kingston to Cornwall. 401. weeping
willows along the road. doing that highway job.
tractor-mower, slow scorching miles, cutting
the thick grass, bottles, tins.

a red car stopped in the shade. a woman,
sun-glasses up on her hair, sitting under a tree.
I stop.

car's okay. only
tired of driving she says. words
get drowned, the big transports
blasting by, clanging their loads of steel.
why don't we go where it's quiet I say
and we climb the fence, thread the tight cedars,
puddles of sun and cicadas here.
the traffic suddenly far.

I run my hands over her arms and legs
under her skirt and jersey. cool heavy flesh.
she steps leaving her underpants in the grass
bends lifting her skirt and I zip loose
grab her hips, slide hot softness
over me, no
holding back, she
calls it right up out of the bones of my toes,
knees, pelvis, small of the back
arching into her deeper deeper

she spins away now dancing
into the solid sun, oh Jesus
August! alone up here like a rat in a hole, three
sleeping bags over my head, the hail,
the wind lifting the roof. Ontario Ontario!
sweet summer's body.
sweet willows.

• some brainless myth. the value of
loneliness. the place to be is where
nobody goes. trendy inversion.
my terra nova: this windy corner.
ice and wreckage for treasures. idiot grin.

trying to lift the blank mask
of this smothered island. there *must*
be a reason why there's nothing here.

and I see it.

the ground is solid rock. the clouds are solid rock.
the trees are solid rock. the snow is solid rock.
the sea is solid rock. the sun is solid rock.
the air is solid rock. the rain is solid rock.
the night is solid rock. the wind is solid rock.

★ ★ ★

all I've written so far: one
message in a bottle.
HELP! GET ME OFF THIS ROCK!

•
rain stops just
in time for a bit of sunset to
break through and

like me,
cooped up so long, all
the birds are down at the beach
stretching their wings in the red light
grabbing a bite before dark.

grey-chested and
the size of a horse's head
one crow
picks his rolling way on foot over
the low-tide stones
slips on kelp
like me
hops
heavily, wings hunched up.

tilting his blue-steel beak
he lifts the odd strand of weed to
peck and sample
or only cocks a cool eye.

no struggle for survival here.

like me
this boy's just out for an evening stroll.

• Looking back I'd say it was the trees that did me in. The image in my mind of shady avenues. At least a leafy screen, I thought, to hide the building fronts, the pink and turquoise plywood faces, bits of fake brick siding here and there and tiny windows high and far apart. The place a horror to me at the start, though that was never what I said. 'High-spirited' and 'unpretentious' were the words I used. And I was in my power then, carrying the gospel to the hinterland, and even though the council boys were skeptical, they figured maybe I knew something that they didn't know. And the novelty of spending money for the sake of beauty took them by surprise, even made them feel a little proud and heady, as though they'd been persuaded to erect an opera house. Only Patey told me outright that they wouldn't grow, the ground too stony everywhere. 'And how do you know?' I asked. 'Has anybody tried before?' And that shut them up, none of them wanting to be a hick or advocate of ugliness. And I went ahead and spent – God even now it makes be blush – fourteen thousand dollars just on digging holes, and had two hundred eight-foot maple trees shipped in. The cost! The cost of that in a place that only two years earlier had finished getting water lines put in. I had no *notion* of the waste and the stupidity, striding up and down seeing how the work was getting on. Milliken Harbour: twin city of Niagara-on-the-Lake. What surprises me now looking back is how many people went along with me, eager to share my vision of a genteel town, eager to have faith in what I knew.

We got them in the ground by late October, their trunks neatly bound in burlap, wooden stakes beside each one, even chicken wire wrapped around the Christly things, and with the early snow drifting down I stood and pictured how they'd look in leaf the following spring, their rustling crowns in rows above the sidewalks of the town. And the snow kept coming and coming all November and December and I'd never seen anything like it, wind piling the drifts right to the roofs on Karden Street, and the council plough was out two or three times a day tumbling the five-ton boulders of snow over my trees. The same guy driving the plough who drove the backhoe when we planted them. And I started to see the logic in bareness and ugliness.

Nobody said much to me about the trees, then or at any time after that. Some old folks would stop me and ask, 'Well how does ya tink yer trees is enjyin de cloimit down ere?' And others would say, 'Niver ye moind dat moi son. Dey'll spring right back up in de spring, good as new.' They all went into use at least, those pampered sticks raised in the chocolate-cake loam of southern Ontario. I saw a lot of them turned into nice hardwood handles for gaffs, the men taking them out on the ice to use on seals. The women got their share too, employing them to prop their clotheslines up. And the kids used some for fishing poles and spears. The rest went into fences and stoves – kindling, cups of tea, meals.

Funny how little was ever said to me. But that was the last big thing I tried.

Which was an even bigger mistake.

•
good weather.
the heavy machinery is quiet.
I climb the eastern bluffs, walk
onto the blasting-grounds
the anvils, the thousand-ton stamp-hammer beds.

acres of stone
mute white
pounded deep into shock.

but sitting down I notice
rammed into crannies
drifted in ash, small
coals, charred tangles of wire
are sprouting leaves,

birds dart,
bees meander through
testing:
green. rustling. seeping up

- Cutting wood today in a fine rain I suddenly thought I could smell my wife's perfume.

 The scent, which was surprisingly distinct, seemed to be coming from the southwest corner of the cabin, near the door. I sniffed like a bloodhound, smelling the cabin wall, the steps, the ground, my clothes, without being able to find where it was coming from.

 After a time the scent faded out, and I went back to cutting wood.

• the weedy path past my door, the skeleton
houses: first,
last things I see in a day.

my only company here: absent people, gaps
where they would have walked, worked,
stood in their doors.

questions, vanished things, are
solid facts
as large as the hills, the fitful bay.

3

•
ducks swoop low over the
near beach as I breast the tall
weeds, stepping
carefully among the spiky planks
around these broken dwellings.

no doors attached, no
glass in the windows, I look in
on fallen ceilings, iron beds, chairs
crushed under avalanches of lath.

where have they gone
the people who carved the air here
with their births and funerals
their scurried visits along the windy paths?

where have their children scattered to?

the grass still rustles with their parents' voices,
people who tried to balance their homes
between water and air.

•
Nels

This one spring an iceberg come and set right on top of Aaron Shale's salmon net. He was in a state about that of course, but there wasn't a thing he could do. After a few days though, the berg foundered, turned bottom-up, and there was Aaron Shale's salmon net away up in the air, draped over the very tip of the thing.

When Aaron saw that he just turned around and went and got an axe. Then he rowed up to the berg all by hisself and climbed aboard of her. The other men were gathered around in their boats watchin – most of 'em scared even to go near the thing lest she broke or rolled again – and they watched Aaron Shale climb the side of that berg like a mountaineer, hackin out step after step for hisself as he went on up to the very pinnacle. Sixty feet over the water. And he unhooked his net and got it down out of there.

•
not only the beach-rock road
(a hedge of alders now, snaking
the salt flats, skirting the shore),
not only the faint village trails
are paths leading your feet, guiding
your eyes to reconstruct the hill-
walls, the sea-windows and doors
that housed these people's lives,

the graves too are paths,
the fallen church is a path,
the tangled gardens, wind-hollow
houses are paths you can't help
following

• who were these people?
what did they make of this place?
were they always thinking of somewhere else as
home? Ireland, St. John's, clattering streets, sun?
was this a break, a long side-loop in their lives?
a chance to get rich on fish?
a way to survive until something better beckoned?
were they lost? baffled? blown here they didn't
know how?
were they home here, planted and satisfied, Eden's
humble attempters? the cod and ducks and berries
limits to the only world they hungered for?

so little left to speak for them.
white stones in the boggy burying ground, a few
small houses fallen in. rich plots of weeds.
a path leading nowhere under the gulls.

what about it, you young girls, you old women?
what did you dream at night with the fire out
and wind tugging the roof?
ice? an ocean of ice closing the island round?
green glimmering mountains grinding the island down?

was it summer you dreamt of? split fish spread in
the sun? dresses and shoes for Sunday paths?
courting in meadows? bells in the blue air?
your babies, your sweet curly-heads, their tiny
fingers clinging?

was it wood stacked in a shed you saw, the stove
fat and red? your family's faces around the supper
lamp, their backs a wall to the night?

whatever you dreamed, you are gone.

your dreams gone too.

• today a sadness in the light itself
the silence
the any-direction-you-want-to-take day

I swim in sadness
breathe it
walk through it like a diver
in some still lagoon

the sadness of things stalled in the earth
with its normal naps and ecstasies

always pain and roughness
right in the clear flow of love

some black root that feeds
on perfect weather.

my children. my family.
their talk, the ways their bodies
pull my blood across the emptiness

• This morning two fishermen came ashore to get drinking water from the spring. I stepped outside to meet them, and they set their tall buckets down, willing to chat. Cyril Wellon, the skipper, a short thick man with spattered spectacles, was full of talk. His brother, Ambrose, nodded and grinned. I invited them in for tea, and they shifted and shuffled at first, caught in the midst of the day's work, threatened with hospitality. As they came in the door they ducked and smoothed their hair and seemed to think of their dirty hands and rubber clothes, as though expecting something fancy or foreign. Lace doilies. China cups. The sight of the tools and decoys put them at ease, and they took a good look around, praising the cozy nook I had for myself.

They wanted to know what I was doing of course, and I asked about their work – three cod traps in the island's coves – and about catches, the price of fish, the number of trips they make. They drank one mug of tea each then had to go, their brothers on the ship no doubt wondering where they'd gotten to.

• it's enough to record
what's obvious.
here in the foreground.

but always this is what's
hardest to see.

the habit of straining your eyes
craning to get above obstacles
is the biggest obstacle.

the doubt that there's any value
in daily things.

• Cyril and Ambrose were by again today and gave me a 'small' codfish – small enough to feed a small family. They had to get back they said, so we stood outside in the light rain and gazed at the bay, curtains of drizzle drifting out of the south, everything soft and still. I asked if they'd known Carm at all or any other people who used to live here. 'Carm? Oh yes, I know Carm,' Cyril said, without even grinning or showing any surprise that I should ask. 'I knew most of the folks one time. I was born over there,' he said, pointing across the harbour. 'Lived there till I was twenty-six. Third from the church. Place isn't standing now.' Nor is the church, I noticed. Always people pointing to where they lived, seeing elaborate structures I can't see. Just grass and rock looking secretive. Everything you do swallowed so fast here. Everything taken away. I wonder, does that make life seem long? Looking back, your childhood world vanished, no beginning to life, no clear markers to measure by, maybe you'd feel you've always been here. Or maybe you'd feel you've never been anywhere.

But these people don't measure by what you see. They carry the world around in their heads. All this rock and water is only a backdrop. Like a felt board to which they attach the cut-out figures in their minds.

Baked the cod on a large griddle. Been eating it all night. Big curved flakes of meat, packed in like feathers, as Elizabeth Bishop says. Enough here for two days if it keeps.

- An eerie feeling when you're fishing a brook and you glance up and notice the tall peak of an iceberg jutting over a hill. On blue sunny days their slab sides blaze unnaturally white, and having forgotten they were there you suddenly see them as giant polar bears craning their necks to spy on you. Shamans' creatures. Come from a far time.

●
I walk around the cabin, the stage
and wharf of Carm Denny, the last
man to live on the island. out here
years after everyone else had gone.
first with his mother, and then she
died and their place burned down
and he stayed on in this hut by the shore
until the police came and took him away.

I lift the latch and step into
the slatted shade of his stage.
cracks and flashing water underneath.
everything still strong and neat.
good hand-cut timbers. wire
and poles and bits of iron scrap
all sorted and stacked or
hung along the walls.
a lifetime of saving this and that.

the dark-stained cutting table
stands by a wall, its top
hollowed and curved as a woman's back.
a little trap door opens to
empty the offal into the waves.
all nicely arranged for gutting his catches
out of the weather.

and where is he now? shot full
of sedative in some bed or chair.
nothing at all in his head or hands.
his life, his whole work broken off
smashed by our superior tidiness
as though it's a favour to him to have
stopped him from meeting once and for all

whatever was hunting him
or on some blue winter day
letting the ringing hills be
the very last bit of what he knew.

•
at times
when dark has fallen
and the wind sea and rain stomp the
earth and cabin walls to another crescendo
I know the door is about to burst in with
some monster

some mountain thunderball screaming
ripping splinters splattering teeth
bone-chips bloody clots of hair.

Carm Denny
who loved this island
and lived alone with its grinding voices
must have expected the same,
guarding his house with charms
blacking his windows at night
to hide himself.

what else could such cold crags
such heaving water intend?

• *Nels*

Now Carm there. There was nothin the matter with the man. Some people talk about him bein mental. He was just shy was all. And he done things his own way. Kept a tidy place he did, worked hard, made first class fish, and he didn't trouble a soul.

He was always fresh shaved when I seen him. And his clothes was clean. There was nothin mental about the man at all.

-
Carm

The warm spring is what done it. Snow all gone from around the house in April month, flies thick on the windows sooner than I'd ever seen before, and this one day I kept getting a queer smell. Garbage and stuff I'd heaved outside I figured, going bad in the sun. I noticed the smell most right in the house, though, and that should of gave me a clue, but I was busy with this and that and didn't think much of it. That night I couldn't sleep, the stink was so fierce. And all at once I remembered. *The ducks!* The dozen or so ducks I still had, skinned and cleaned from the ones I got in the winter. I had them froze out in the pantry in a big wooden tub. At least they *used* to be froze. That damn south wind. So I lit a candle and went to the pantry and lifted the lid of the tub, and the stink that came out of there belted me like a loose boom, and there was a white flash at my hand and the next thing I knew I was down on my arse on the kitchen floor with a dozen skinned ducks zipping around the room with long blue flames shooting out of their hind ends.

I thought I was seeing stars until one of them whooshed by so close it burnt away half my hair. They were smacking the walls and falling and taking off again like balloons when you blow them up and let them go. I saw one shoot under the daybed and two or three stopped on the ceiling spinning round and round, and one bust through the window shade and that peeled up in a skin of flame, and I watched the bird streaking off in a long blue spiral over the island hills like it had come to life again and gotten free. And by now the curtains were blazing away and the daybed too and I jumped up and got out of there just in my long underwear.

In an hour the house was gone. I had to go right down to the shore because of the heat. The walls and roof lifted up with a roar like burning wings, everything inside blinding red, table and chairs, cupboard and stove, everything, every bit standing just like I left it, but made of red coal. Glowing. And you could see through it all like glass. Even my coat on the hook was a mesh of red wire.

And then it came down.

Soundless. And I had to fall in the water to keep from being burnt too and the sparks and spinning bits climbed straight up the sky. All I owned. All my people had ever owned.

• the wind is so strong
has so many tricks
so many ways of knocking the cabin around
so many voices
I start to think it's a person.

outside
squatting to shit
I'm nervous with all the leaping
and battering going on
I glance over my shoulder
half expecting the wind
to be standing there grinning
ready to kick my arse.

● down bag over my head
I lie curled, teeth clenched
wanting to sleep, not
give a damn. wind
batters the place
raises boards and shingles like
feathers on some ass-backwards hen,
kicks the cabin wall, bulges it in,
here comes the window I think
(like lying four feet in front of a cannon
loaded with broken glass)
spikes, rafters creak, jerk
there goes the roof
the whole sky's black torrent grabbing in,
the cabin jolts, jumps like a cart
we're up in the air I think
head for Oz, the
wall staggers, nearly sits on me,
here comes the window, a glass
dam bursting splinters and sleet

●

I come out of sleep, a crack of light at the door smoothly growing, Mrs Brake's head poking in: 'Mister.... Mister. ... You awake? I knows I said ya could have the room to yerself. But Jewelleen's come back. Stay put now, stay put. If ya doesn't mind her I'll not charge y'a thing in the mornin.'

What the hell now?

She's gone. Whispers in the hall and a girl comes in, tight cashmere sweater, long hair she tosses over her shoulder, a wind of warm neck perfume hitting me as she turns and sits on the bed to unzip her boots.

I stay on my side watching her pull and kick things off then lift her arms letting a nightgown slide down her slim back. Burrowing under the blankets she says, 'You keep over there.'

Which is easier said than done, the way this bed sags. Like sleeping on the rim of a giant bowl. I turn my face to the wall, hook a knee and elbow over the mattress edge and try to doze.

* * *

'Oof! You're crushin me!' Someone shoving my face and chest. Jewelleen! Smooth soft limbs struggling under me. 'Sorry,' I say.

I try to get off, drawing my left thigh out from between her legs, over a firm pelvic arch, groping for something to push against, not there, sorry, there. I push, heave over, roll up the slope, grapple back on the rim.

* * *

'Mmmp!' This time I'm on the bottom, wake up with her mouth just under my eye, a thin trickle of spit in my ear. She shifts, spreads hair in my face, slides warm solid legs down mine, toes combing my ankles, and feeling her long bareness, I check gently, finding her nightie all pulled up, run that hand over the fine down of her legs. Her hip's high cliff. Her low waist.

She snuggles closer to me. 'Didn't you bring no pajamas?'

- This place is wet all the time. The bushes, the long grass always sopping with recent rain. Two steps and your legs are drenched. The plume of one stalk of grass, one clump of buttercups holds enough water to leave a large patch of your trousers soaking wet. Your shoes squish when you put them on.

• on the wind-shaken wharf
a second time
I haul up my improvised trap
(onion sack on a rusty barrel hoop.
sculpin bait. stone weight)
the first time only a crab
had been dining there. he backed
away snipping the air and
dropped between the planks.

but here!
dripping out of the waves: winkles!
big and surprisingly *green*!

I rush them to the crackling stove
(bless you and thank you, many of
your kind have died in this manner
previously) and boiling brine.
then hook them spiralling
slick and rubbery
out of their shells, slice them
into the skillet
popping with garlic.

ah! sweet luxury.
though it rains
and the cabin staggers into the
darkening wind.

Reading Matter

> SOUL IN SALT
> Reflections on Newfoundland
>
> by
> Stuart Patterson

Purgatory and Penal Servitude

The people of Newfoundland have always had a profound sense of the fallen nature of this world and a vivid understanding of the concept of purgation. This psychological predisposition has given them an affinity for the Catholic faith and for the beliefs of certain fundamentalist Protestant sects; but religious indoctrination is not the source of the Newfoundlander's refined understanding of punishment and sin. It springs, instead, from his relationship with his environment and from his general notion of the history of British and Irish emigration to the 'new worlds' of America, Australia, and New Zealand.

Newfoundlanders know that while convicts, remittance men, lepers, and the superfluous poor of Britain were being shipped off against their will to the sunny shores of Virginia and New South Wales, the ice-shrouded shores of Newfoundland were out of bounds to emigrants: not only were convicts *not* sent here (the British government perhaps feeling there had to be some limit to the severity of its laws), but settlement was actually *forbidden*. Nevertheless, our Newfoundland forefathers, defying the authority of the British crown and the might of the British navy, chose to shun any association with those convict colonies to the south and in a spirit of stalwart independence elected to establish their homes and the homes of their helpless descendants among the rocks, bogs, sleet, and blackflies of this free northern isle.

From the first, Newfoundlanders have been a wrongheaded, stubborn, defiant, eccentric, and self-defeating people. And through the succession of generations, by means of a process of natural selection, these traits have been accentuated and strengthened in those individuals who have chosen to stay in their island home. But even so, in the midst of his proud and crotchety ruminations, gazing over the boulders and slob-ice of his ancestral domain, the modern Newfoundlander cannot escape the quiet, nagging question: 'What in the name of bloody Jesus did my great-great-grandad have to go and choose this arse-end of a place for, instead of Brisbane or Tampa?' It could not have been that his forefathers were all lunatics or elaborate pranksters, he knows, or that their bodies' thermometers weren't working, or that the climate has changed, or that they were all allergic to vegetation, or suffered from asthma and found relief in the fog.

No. The Newfoundlander has a vague but powerful sense that other factors – moral factors – were at work in leading his precursors here. While temporal legislators in Britain were busy sending social misfits off to Australia, another, higher, *eternal* law was mysteriously at work sending those guilty of profounder sins to a profounder punishment in Newfoundland – sending them through the miraculous and ironic agency of their own 'free' wills.

But what could the sins of our parents have been? Clearly, not mere murders and thefts of bread. They must have sinned in some deep and obscure manner, perhaps against life itself, perhaps through cynicism or ingratitude or pride. No Newfoundlander believes in the romantic image of the pioneer, the image of wholesome lads and lasses ambitiously quitting the Old World to find their fortunes in the new-found-land. Even if he knows his personal forebears were exceptions to the rule, he feels that his cultural ancestor, as a type, sailed out and away from the civilized world with the brand of the condemned man burned more deeply and more certainly into him than into any convict ever exiled to Australia.

Each Newfoundlander thus harbours within him a sense of having sprung from and been born into a kind of voluntary penal colony. For him the world is certainly no paradise – thorns and thistles are the least of his troubles (in fact he'd do handsprings if he could get a few to grow) – and he must constantly struggle with the question of why the choice of such a world was made and why he cannot change it or leave it for a better one. Inevitably, consciously or unconsciously, the Newfoundlander comes to the conclusion that he is paying for something, that he is being purged of some deep and terrible sin.

Aristocracy

Those who fail to understand Newfoundland often criticize its inhabitants for not caring about the appearance of their landscape and their public places. They point to the mutilated remains of cars and trucks which line the roadways and crowd the front yards of most homes; they point to the broken glass and rubbish that litter the beaches, the playgrounds and parking lots; they point to the mangled forests and to the unfinished houses with weathered particle-board on show. And they conclude from all this that Newfoundlanders are sloppy people.

What they do not understand is that the Newfoundlander perceives the whole of the external world as hopeless, irredeemable chaos. A few more forsythia shrubs, a bit less broken glass, a dab or two of paint can't make a jot of difference one way or another in a world which is constantly trampled by stampeding elephants, ravaged by fire, scoured by glaciers and tidal waves, and pillaged by hoards of sex-crazed Zulus, metaphorically speaking.

People in even the most orderly and polished societies tacitly accept the fact that there are some areas and some processes in the physical world which are, for practical reasons, beyond beautification. No one, in even the highest culture, worries about what sewer pipes look like on the inside or troubles himself with the abattoir's decor. Few people anywhere vacuum their flower gardens or count it a disgrace that the soles of their shoes and the tires of their cars must sometimes get muddy. Having done their best with the manageable portions of the world, they agree to ignore, with dignity and aplomb, those unmanageable parts that remain.

In Newfoundland, we are simply looking at a different ratio between manageable and unmanageable components. Out of necessity the Newfoundlander has had to relinquish responsibility for everything beyond his kitchen and parlour – and in some cases, for everything beyond his kitchen alone. Outside of that stable and controllable realm, all is wilderness. The ocean, the climate, and the flinty land see to that.

The measure of the refinement of a people cannot lie in the *amount* of the world they have organized and beautified, for in this case the refinement of peoples and the achievement of civilizations would be directly propor-

> tionate to the manageability of the environments they inhabit. And we know that this is not the case. Some of the most deplorable savages have inhabited – and still do inhabit – some of the most temperate regions of the earth.
>
> The measure of the refinement of a people – the test of the aristocracy of the human spirit, so to speak – must lie in the extent to which a people have cherished and beautified those manageable areas which are available to them, and in the grace with which they ignore and absolve themselves from the rest.
>
> On this basis, it might be argued that Newfoundlanders are the earth's most aristocratic people, for they manage with consummate grace their tiny kitchens and parlours, and dismiss with superb nonchalance all the rest of the universe.

What kind of crap is this? Some prancing academic in his Mozart clothes.

I lift the stove lid and stuff the book in, then move the kettle up to catch the heat.

An outboard noise. Out the window, Cyril brings his boat in behind the windy wharf. Good. Burn the thing to boil him a cup of tea.

-
Cyril

We was froze in seven months of the year out here. There was no comin or goin then sir. Except for the time Frank Tobin walked over the ice to Englee for the mail. A day out and a day back. Seen it myself. He come in over the tickle there, the mail bag froze right to him. He'd been into the water once or twice, and he lifted his arm and wanted to give a cheer, but his moustache was froze that thick he couldn't open his mouth. But that was only one man ever done that, and he was lucky I'd say, with the ice shiftin and shovin around out there every day. It *might* be solid across for a couple hours, then it might be a couple miles of rough sea, or maybe you'd drift away on a big pan, or a storm come up and you'd wander off the wrong way. That's fifteen miles of the worst kind of ice for half the year. So you was stuck see. And you wanted things laid up in advance. There was the salt fish you'd made in the summer, and some would order a barrel of salt meat, and there was a scattered rabbit or partridge you'd get in on the height of land, but ducks was the big thing in the winter. Ducks! My son, you'd never see the like of the ducks here in the wintertime. The shoal water out there where it don't freeze is where they come down. In their thousands. And their tens of thousands!

Usually at twilight it'd be. Down and down they'd come and you'd wonder where in the name of God they was all comin from. Out of a winter sky like that with nothin around but ice for so many miles. And as they come down they'd all be callin at once. Not quack quack quack or whatever you'd think. But callin together like that the sound is somethin you'd never dream could come from a duck. Big and loud as the wind, but real high. A bit like a howl and a bit like a scream, and it rises and falls, rises and falls in waves, and it's comin from everywhere. Not just from the ducks. But from under the ice. From behind you. From over the hills. The whole sky seems to be howlin, howlin. Closin in.

The first time I heard it I was only a youngster then and it made me cry. Not because I was scared. It just sort of hauled the sobs up out of me. It was the sound of food for one thing I guess. But there's more to it than that. Anyway, we'd load up our guns, old muzzle-loaders, and get out on the ice as close to the open water as we could. Then we'd lie flat on our backs and wait for the ducks to come in over us. I'll never forget this one time. It was fierce cold. Thirty below. And a wind comin down from the nor'west. My father, my uncle, my cousin Eustace and me went out just before nightfall, a good half-mile over the ice and lay down at the edge of the lead. I'd of been about seventeen at the time. Eustace, he was my best chum then, was a year older than me. He'd been ailin a lot that winter. Coughin blood. Well we lay there with the snow driftin over us and got our guns set. We used to put everythin into those guns for shot. Nuts, bolts, nails and such. I'd been scoutin around for somethin to use in mine that time and my grampa said to me look how'd this be, and he got his gold pocket-watch that hadn't worked for a year or more. Salt was into it he said, no use keepin the thing around. So he took it apart with a hammer and shears and fed all the little wheels and springs down the muzzle of my gun. Dropped the hands in last and rammed in a bit of brin. That oughta bring you luck he said.

So I was lyin there feelin my body freeze and prayin I'd soon be able to blow the b'jesus out of a dozen or so ducks when finally I heard the howlin, way off first, and they started comin down out of the dark. The first ducks always come straight down on the open lead and the ones after them swing round in the air and hold up a bit and then come down on the backs of the ones that are already pitched, and the ones after them do the same. In waves like. Howlin and singin like Judgment Day. It takes a long time for them all to get landed. And those that are still comin in don't head for the open water at the edge of the lead, they just keep wheelin round and comin down in the centre, ducks on ducks on ducks and the crowd of them spreads out on the water like molasses pourin out of a jug. When the flock swung round so it was comin down over us, we all let fly up into them. Four long flames and I said goodbye to my grampa's watch, and all the other ducks went off the open water again breakin one another's necks in mid air.

Ninety-seven birds we got at the one time. And you take what you get with the one shot, cause there's no loadin again with your hands froze. We were up then dodgin about, gettin the ducks into the sacks we'd been lyin on, and in the dark I didn't notice at first that Eustace wasn't doin the same as the rest of us. I went over to him, and he was lyin there half covered with ducks. He was stone dead. Already nine parts froze. The funny thing was he'd fired his gun along with the rest of us. The kick of the old bitch must of knocked the last bit of breath out of him.

•

the cold rooms. morning, the fire out. ice
in the bucket. clothes stiff on a chair. day
and night the same wool next to the skin. the
long touching of naked bodies only in summer,
years away, another life, a dream. will will
will moving the stiff limbs. setting to work.

bad food. little food. fever in bed. under a
slow tide. hot. cold. poker clanking, kitchen
voices floating above. sky-wind, snow-desert
circling circling, shaking the thin walls.
stillness in here. a warm pool. warm sinking.
man a little thing. death a little thing.

● what can we do in such elements?

rock hills only recently
softened with green, some moss
and boggy hollows

vast migration of cloud

the wind an invisible glacier
wearing the island down

I keep warm burning
bits of a house

the work of people who tried to live here.

• Families so strong around here, blood lines making a human net to hold these capes and islands in, brothers working together, fathers and sons, sisters married but still in touch around the cove, their children running together, it makes me odder still in their eyes – and in my own eyes too, a fragment blown out of the nation's centre, wife and children gone, brother a stranger thousands of miles away. To the Wellons I must lack substance, dignity, to care so little for my kind, wandering here alone, family history effaced, lost in anonymous routines. What's there to tell them about? How my father, one of the few people I have the power to help, waits for a call or letter from me, some sign that his bloody useless son remembers him? Oh I do. I remember him all the time. Wherever I go. Galt Brass. Words under my nose every day somewhere, schools, bars, garages, ships. Tried to tell him once: in my most private moments I am reminded of you. Didn't see the humour. But it isn't completely untrue, and it isn't completely a joke. Even in Englee for Christ sake, the tavern, I pushed through the plywood door marked men leaving the heavyweight ladies' dart league stomping and roaring behind, and stood for a quiet moment taking a pee, humming, pleasantly bombed, miles away from the guys I'd been yakking with, and there over the urinal the solid brass valve and elbows beaded with sweat and Galt Brass stamped in the nickel plate, and the unavoidable memories stamped in me. Like always when I'm most vulnerable, called to a minute's silence in honour of. My father bent at his lathe, the blackened panes overhead, his lunchpail, coveralls, in and out of the steel gates every day since he was 16, except for the years in the war, and he's been there what? 43 years by now and won't get a rest till the day he's 65. And then what? With his loneliness, his empty time? Life used up in boredom and sweat, the brass ribbons curling under his hands, tons and tons of fittings and valves, enough to bury this island, his patient hands, partly for me, I know that, partly in hope his son would find something better to do. Usual thing. And I've disappointed him, also the usual thing. Going to Newfoundland sweet Jesus Christ have you ever heard anything like it? The place they're always moving away from! Taking my education off to the farthest corner of nowhere. Wasting my time. And his 43-year sacrifice. Making a failure of his failure. The usual thing. The very thing I'll be damned if I'm going to do! Have my kids see me the same: stuck and timid and sacrificed 'for them.'

Maybe my family ties are stronger than it looks, only twisted and stretched in strange ways. And I wish he could see that. What I'm doing here. That I'm trying to stop wasting our time.

•
From this distance, Karen, so many clear facts: that I've been dead and giving you nothing now for years, and it runs in my mind, the break, the break, how close it was, and it strikes me all at once that this *is it!* That it's here. What am I doing off on an island anyway? You're gone and I won't get you back and I want to run into the ocean and swim to the nearest airport as fast as I can. But I know that's wrong. (It goes around like this.) I know I'm digging life out of this place. I hope for all of us.

• the things you look at
look at well.
the plants and rocks and sea.

every move a deliberate one.
meals and washing plates
and getting wood.

the thoughts: not
stuffed down in you like socks in a bag
but parts of the landscape now, regions you
pass through:
thickets or barrens or open shore.

and always the background pull
an aching magnet inside you:
home.
sweet lives. sweet
bodies against you

- The cemetery. I notice how many graves of children there are. Lists of children often on one stone with a phrase preserving their parents' love and sorrow. This hits like an axe. Especially looking up from the small marble plaques to the few ruins, the sea.

I feel very near these people. Life's lonely effort so plain here.

Also a kind of duty to them. Since I've made myself their guest, though likely the most ignorant one they've had, not knowing who they were. All I see is where they lived and that they died here and were left behind. But I feel the need to tell this if I can.

4

• The coarse grass growing around the cabin draws its life from a layer of black peat three or four inches deep at the most. Below that are stones and pure sand. I cut squares of turf with an old splitting knife, stab, claw the tangled wads free. The smell that rises is raw and sour – faint bog fumes, wet minerals – the end of some slow process having little to do with the history of animals. I tear the clumped roots, examining them. Prod the exposed earth, turning the grains with my knife. No bugs or grubs. Nothing wriggling or digging or scampering. The few worms I find are thin match-sized things, anemic, nearly white. Not enough to go over a hook.

I look in various places – high spots, wet spots, under moss, under weeds – I lift stones and pieces of wood, all the fisherman's tricks. At one of the fallen houses I guess where the door would have been and dig, imagining kitchen scraps, dogs, people pissing, serenading the stars, the whole fertile trail of life. But whatever there was to eat here has been eaten long ago and the worms have starved or moved on. Resettled like everyone else. My only hope is the house most recently used. I straighten my back, take my knife and jar and walk the half mile to Carm Denny's shack.

And here, before Carm's door, under the first plank I turn: blood-brown worms, fat, quickly contracting like tendons suddenly laid bare. I move fast too, getting most of them.

Bent, I circle the building grubbing and rooting. Every shingle and stick I lift yields bait. Things Carm ate and didn't eat, turned to worms. A kind of organic shadow of the man. A lingering aura of his heat and movements stirring in the sod. The worms feeding under his window at night when he was here, curling and drawing themselves through years of what he had thrown away, sliding into the sound of his humming, his lonely talk, into and out of the warm rectangle of light that lay in the grass.

And I feel a bond of brotherhood with Carm, as though I am

touching some extended parts of him, veins that had spread from his body taking root in the land from which he had never divided himself. I move swiftly, borrowing his life, his island's life, feeling it coiling, pulsing under my hands.

•
Cyril

The last time I saw Carm was end of September a year ago. Last trip out for the season for us. We'd taken our traps up and I went along over to see how he was set for the winter, tell him we wouldn't be back till spring. Everything fine he said, lots of fish and flour and whatnot, startin to haul wood. Garden okay. So we talked a bit and I said well mind the women don't run away with you out here. I liked to rib him about that since he was always sayin he'd seen women walkin around the cove. He chuckled a bit sort of shy-like the way he did, then he come up close to me and he says right serious, Cyril, he says, I want to warn you. Don't come ashore here no more. Stay on your boat and keep her out in the bay. The cliffs, he said, and he pointed to all them big rocks up behind you here, the cliffs are all gonna come crashin into the harbour any day. And he looked at me that strange sir I swear his eyes didn't have no colour in them, no centre to them at all.

•
Carm

Two more women. Size of crows now, crossing the eastern head. Taking the shore path. Where the hell they coming from I'd like to know. What are they looking for?

Big women, these two, black dresses and shawls, and they keep their backs straight. One fat by the look of it, broad, heavy-built with a black bonnet on. The other one thin, hair in a bun. Side by side up from the shore. Hard bitches. Hiding their cunts under their clothes like trained dogs. Secret weapons. Sisters I bet. Proud of their wickedness. Right by my window without looking in. They know I'm here though. They know I'm here. Pocky face on the big one like a leg of pork, small bullet eyes straight ahead. Skin sucked into the skull holes on the other, mouth open like she breathed in strong stink and couldn't breathe out again. I stay right still. Make one sign, go close to them and I know what happens, skin and black clothes drop down and those scraggy jackals come snapping up under me ploughing their steel snouts in deep, dragging my shit tubes out in front of my eyes.

They walk by to the west. Two stiff backs. Down into the gulch, and I watch to see them come up the other side. But they don't. Not for the half hour I wait. Grass blowing. Rock across the gulch going dark and light, dark and light. The crucifix then and the rest of it! Guardians at every point, the best I've got, seal this place so tight they can't get close. Bible on that windowsill to cover the sea. Bread and a medal facing the land. Face of Our Lord and money for there, statue and rosary looking west, quick, coins in the windows upstairs, and I'm down again with the gun and out in the wind hanging the cross on the closed door last thing.

Across to the edge of the gulch. I look down.

Nothing. Tide stones and puncheon staves. Tricked! Tricked! Tricked! They've gone around by the shore back to the house. Probably watched me coming here,

I turn quick, the long grass diving flat, the house going dark, dark and light. Or they slipped into the rock seam under me. That's how it looks. Entered the stone sideways, walked through it like killers at night. Rock devils is what they are. Out of the island's gut.

• jagged island.
island of noise.
the sea serious as ever, breaking
all that it touches.
wind tearing itself to pieces
pounces with all its weight, stops, flattens
grass again. tramples the waves.

the mountains cinder grey
cinder jagged
handsome as animals
hunt the passing clouds.
gathering trouble.

- Walked to the old settlement and visited three houses I hadn't seen before, ones overlooking French Cove. The ground is high there and the houses large, noble. Statements of grace and ownership. Now of course the windows and doors are empty sockets. Great rents gape in the walls, and the sea, sky and rough hills show through. Have eaten through. The way stones wear out shoes and water eats through steel.

Approaching the first house I sensed what the ghosts of the place were thinking, and I felt foreign, ashamed, standing there with my knapsack and fishing rod and camera. I left my things in the grass and stepped through the doorway into a colourless space. Among fallen ceilings and shelves. Lost life. Labour nothing can call back. The torture of being deserted given form. An abandoned child built these walls with its cries.

But a tough skeleton too. The core of what happened here. Calm talk of the people nailing the rafters up. A clapboard shell. Holding their lives in the winter wind.

- I decided to move into Carm's cabin yesterday. His place is closer to good fishing and has a roof without leaks and a better stove. Devoted the day to carrying things here and tidying up – though surprisingly little of that to do: some bean tins and candle ends left by visitors. I already feel completely at home. The building and location make more sense, the windows take in all the shore and bay.

It's like standing inside the head of someone who knows the place.

•
August 15. Lady Day. Tall sun-filled sky over the salt meadows, waves of reeds, the flat islands out from the cove, the wide ocean rim.

Flocks of sea birds constantly rising in white scattering bursts. The black brooks and lagoons busy with ducks.

• not man's time here.
sun's time.
rock's time.
I begin to feel it.

days blink by – light
and cold flowing over – tide
breathing smoothly, evenly, I

slip between half-seconds, flash
light-beam pinball-style, do
ten thousand vanishing things
in a breath.

• I can see it so well, the cafés and bars, Queen Street West, the sun blasting down, the cars and racket, the awnings and railings and chairs, and Karen gay and talking, her sunglasses bouncing the light, her slim tanned arms on the table, her loose top and all the alert men and you can't blame them, a beautiful woman without a man, I can see it so well, friends of her sister, cool professional guys laughing and chatting and asking her out and she goes of course, eager to make friends, she goes with them. But how far does she go? That's what I'd like to know. And how far is she really away? But I see things clearly here and I know they don't have a chance, those poor guys so painfully unconcerned with how they look, so perfectly faded and wrinkled and tanned and scuffed, they don't have a chance because of where they are, and because of where I am – enjoying the most elaborate advantage any lover ever contrived. I'm not just a man anymore. I'm an island. The wind and the smell of space and the animals moving through. And she always liked inaccessible men. And I can't get more inaccessible than this.

Timing though. Timing now is the thing. To not let it drag on too long. Everyone changes in time.

• August 21. all night.

bless me or you'll have to
drag me around forever

bless me or I will not
let you go

bless me or I'll drag
you around forever

bless bless you bless me
around forever

bless me or I will not
let you go

- Steady rain all day and the air still. Sweeping the cabin this morning I lifted a piece of linoleum and found a trap door, the entrance to Carm's root cellar – just a hole in the rock really, neatly packed with peat. All that seemed to be down there at first was mummified potatoes, and then I noticed a biscuit tin set back on a ledge under the cabin floor. Inside the tin was a Bible, and in the Bible a photograph of a girl. I took these up into the light and spent a long time looking at them, wondering why they were there. The girl, seen from the waist up, is standing against a white clapboard wall. She is wearing a kerchief and a dark coat buttoned to the throat. Her hair, where it shows at her forehead and above one shoulder, is black. She is handsome, her face lean, her jaw and cheekbones strong. Her eyes are large and dark by the look of it. But there is no light in her face, no smile, no desire to please. She is not angry, nor is she frightened or withdrawn into herself, but she is guarded all the same. She does not like whoever is looking at her. I would guess she is eighteen or nineteen. There is nothing written on the back.

The red ribbon book mark and the photo were both at the same place in the Bible: Genesis 32, all about Jacob's travels. I thought about keeping the Bible up to read, but finally decided to put it back where I found it, the tin tightly shut and the photo inside.

•
day by day a power
coming out of the rock

my past a theory
my job, my dithering
belong to somebody else

nothing settled yet
everything waits to be seen
but so what?
roll on through it
without coming apart

I am this island now

strong. solid.

• *Carm*

I wasn't always alone like people think. The year after my mother died a boat coming late from the Labrador called in here. Had lost its fresh water in a gale and needed to make repairs, so they anchored in the bay and they used my wharf, and twice they had supper with me. There was a girl among them, had been all summer making fish on the Labrador, and I took a liking to her. She was straight and beautiful and I knew she liked my place by the way she stood at the window, the way she touched the lamp, the chair, and I said to her right out you'll stay with me won't you, and I showed her what I had for the winter, potatoes and turnips under the floor, fish in the stage, flour and butter and that, and showed where my dad's house used to be, the black ashes still there, and I said I was saving to build it up again, a two-storey house with windows over the bay. And she said she'd stay. And the night before they sailed, her uncle who was captain and head of the crew paid her off and married us right here. We put our hands on the Bible, and it was done.

The fish was still running here then and every day I was working bringing them in, and my God that woman could work too, and we scarcely spoke together for over a week. And then one night she started to talk to me. Her father had been a mariner out of Trinity Bay. When she was seven years old he was lost at sea and her mother had no means of keeping her youngsters fed, so they went to the aunts and uncles. Some to St. John's, some to Placentia Bay. Her mother died of consumption when she was ten. She remembered it all so clearly still. The way her mother had cried saying goodbye to her. And she said she hated the uncle that took her in.

That winter didn't last any time at all. She used to go with me everywhere, back over the island for ptarmigan and for timber to ship around in the spring. And at night we'd talk and sing together – and the songs that woman knew! The hundreds of songs she knew! In the spring though she didn't want people to know she was here. If anyone came ashore she'd go and hide. Once we heard voices right close to the house and she quick got into the turnip cellar under the floor. I tried to tell her it didn't matter a sheep's fart, but she wouldn't have people looking at her, people I knew from Conche and Englee is what she meant. I don't know what the reason for that was. By ourselves we were happy as birds.

When the baby was on its way I was some glad. Made a small bed from young spruce and painted it green. A son or daughter, it didn't matter which. The problem was she couldn't be having the baby alone. I said I'd get a woman from Englee when the time was near. But she wouldn't agree. Wanted to go to some people of hers in St. John's. And when a boat bound that way came by they took her along. She told me she'd write, and I was going to go when the season was done and bring her home. And a letter came then after a couple months, a letter her aunt had wrote saying my wife was dead. My wife and our baby both. I went with the man who'd carried the letter out, and got to St. Anthony, and finally a boat from there to St. John's. And I found the house of the aunt. But the woman looked at me like I was lord of the plague. Made me stand in the door and all she would say was my wife and child were buried down to the Belvedere. I went and walked through the rows of crosses and stones, the snow on the ground by then. Her name wasn't anywhere. At the big cathedral I spoke with the man with the books and lists of names and he told me he had no record of her being buried there. The bitch of an aunt didn't want to see me again but I pounded and pounded and made her open the door, and she handed me out a photograph of my wife and said to go back to the graveyard again, that the girl was gone for sure the same as the uncle was. And she shut the door in my face and that was that.

I took the train across the island then, my only time on a train, all the ponds and barrens covered in snow, and I travelled by snow machine and dog team down from Deer Lake to Englee. But nobody wanted to go to the Grey Islands by then with the coves freezing across. I spent the rest of the winter with people in Englee, cutting wood in the bush and mending nets. I never told anyone why I'd been gone. I was waiting, that's all, waiting and seeing my house that I couldn't get back to. Empty. Frozen and dark.

- So far this year the fishermen here haven't been doing too well. They blame the good weather. 'When it's bad on the water, the fishin's good,' Cyril says. 'If the water's calm, the cod seem to get right logy.' So all these boys are actually yearning for storms. This drives me nuts. I tell myself they're just as at home on the water as I am on land. But the danger of drowning is always there. They told me two of their friends died this spring in the water. Overloaded their boat and were swamped. Again this paradox: they were so lucky in their catch it killed them. If they're safe on the water, they're in danger of not making a living. If they're catching a lot of fish, they're in danger of losing their lives.

•
Carm

And the whole time she was talking, telling me where she was from, she had the big kettle of water on the stove and she kept the fire high, getting up from the table every couple of minutes and adding more wood, and the room got hotter and hotter and when she was done with her story she got the tub down off the wall and set it on the floor by the stove and dipped hot and cold water into it and said now I could help her get washed, and she took off her clothes, her body like the cabin breaking, the rock breaking open, the heart of the earth coming out and I'd never seen a woman naked before, and she crouched down in the tub and splashed and rubbed under herself and then she gathered her hair over her shoulder and told me to wash her back and I got to my feet, my head up in the hot air at the ceiling, up with the lamp and I watched myself go and bend down beside her, stretch out my hand like a beetle crawling and all of a sudden its hard back opens and wings come out and it flies away, it was like a nut breaking, the soft white kernel falling into your palm, and I dipped my hand in the water and moved it down her shoulder and spine, down the curve of her hip and her round rear end, and I felt the warmth melting my hand and all my body was melting too, leaking out of the hard shell of my skin, out of my legs, the floor getting farther away and I had to stop then, and I knelt down and put my two hands on her feeling her wet back wondering how could a human body be made of something so soft, how could it stand against the world, and I put my hand down under her to feel what a woman is like, the hot smooth folds into her body, and my fingers were wood, they were canvas gloves I wanted to throw away, and I put my face to her back to feel, my mouth to her shoulders and neck tasting her skin, and she stood then turning, her nipples and belly shaking water over me and she said now you get in and I'll wash you too.

• things here flower
in death

bones and shells
tossed from the sea
sifted out of the stones
are the final disclosures of mulish wills
hidden in life

the spruce, its spine
on the rock, fighting the salt wind
looks more like a mound of moss than a tree
until it lets go of its bark and needles
and reveals
        bone lightning

white tines so hard
so deliberately set they claw
cries and speeches out of the wind, moaning
singing their furious stories years
before they scatter in the rocks

• Was on the water most of the day with the Wellons. Cyril asked three days ago if I'd ever seen a cod trap being pulled, said they'd be by to get me next trip out. I heard their boat at seven this morning and jumped out of bed, no time to eat, went out the door pulling my sweater on and that was the start. Even now, ten at night, the cabin is flowing and tipping, the floor like a breathing belly. I close my eyes and: codfish, body to body, eyes, mouths gaping. Walls of stirring life.

• vast bare plain of galloping animals.
plesiosaurs, ichthyosaurs, dragons,
leviathans, medieval chimeras
shoulder to shoulder herding, charging, *the world
is a monster stampede!*

us
bouncing across their heads and backs.

crazy to try it at all. trusting
a little wooden thing like this.

• these *birds* again. skimming
the water gullies all their lives

dodging the grabbing waves until
they can't.

and that's okay.

slipping into the only thing
they ever looked at

the thing they were only ever
an inch above.

• an adventure for me,
for them it's like taking the bus.
Ambrose and Harold doze on the thwarts
while I hang on low in the bow, my jacket
hood drawn down to my eyes because
the wind off this August water is cold as hell
and the young bull skiff puts
its head into each wave
loving the spray.

cold. wet. silver.
grey. not qualities but
the only things here.
and space.
the whole open Atlantic the same.

and us.

•
up. down. up. down.
cliffs and the burly cove do
giant sit-ups, boards underfoot
shy, dodge, my boots shooting away
in the blood and water (with Cyril
steadily lifting, hauling the line)
I sprawl scramble for someplace to
brace my feet hitting the
engine house I reach out catch
the turning capstan bar – Pete
pushing the other end – I hang on
help twist the capstan creaking around
drawing the trapline tight the long
skiff tipping pressed down with
the weight and nothing giving
nothing coming up the birch capstan
breaks off in our hands the line dives
back into the sea.

'She's some fierce tide,' Cyril says.
He throws the broken capstan into the bow.
'We'll try again in an hour's time.'

• knees on the rolling gunnels
we lean out drawing the trap up slowly
hand over hand, lifting a thousand
fish in a tightening house.

something boiling begins to emerge,
one, two tails turn
swelling the surface, then
long backs braiding smoothly rise
clear to the light as we claw more and more
of their mesh walls away from them.

Cyril is dancing, already guessing
how many thousand pounds as he jabs
the dip net among them yanking
thudding their slippery bodies into the skiff
he digs wildly ripping the air through his
teeth, making a rainbow of fish
white bellies, eyes, mouths
wide with amazement going by in a blur, he
works like a man in a fairy tale
who is shown a mountain of gold
and told he can keep whatever he digs in a day.

• The cod, by the look of them, should be fierce fighters. Their sleek hard bodies, their tunnel mouths show they are meant for chasing and swallowing things. They could sink boats, beat fishermen to death if they chose to thrash and make things difficult. But merely having their motion checked, merely seeing a net, is enough to make these fish decide to die.

They must live too tightly focused, like bullets drilling the sea, a single murderous purpose filling their brains. Or they swim entranced by tiny fins flitting ahead of them. We are possibilities they cannot admit. We have broken the one train of thought they are capable of, and now they wallow sideways to the surface gaping and gulping like sleepwalkers fatally wakened. Even those that have slipped over the net and are free remain too deeply astonished to ever use their gills and dive again.

Astonishment is the ruling temper here. Hundreds of mute mouths hang open. Hundreds of huge eyes appalled at the sky. I stare down at them equally stunned. There is something hypnotic about this naked mass dredged out of the sea, their long forms swelling and fainting, their bellies' fine mail shimmering pink, pearl-white, blue, their backs lit with unsteady greens and browns: colours and shapes themselves confused, not meant for the light, the caustic air. They are burning before our eyes, these liquid animals.

Something moves to my left, I look and Cyril's son Ross is up and stepping over the side of the boat. For Christ sake the boy's trying to walk on them! Cyril sees him in time and shouts, and Ross pulls his green booted leg back into the boat and sits for a minute looking sheepish and dazed as though he too has just been wakened out of a dream.

•
five tons of fish slippery as
pumpkin seeds on the longliner's deck,
I lift my foot high and wade
into them, feeling their bodies press
my sinking legs, stepping
on eyes and bellies, things
I usually treat so carefully.

two splitting tables ready to go,
Cyril gives me a knife and shows
how to slit the throats just
back of the gills then run the
blade down the belly seam to the tail.

I do this, passing the opened fish
to Ross who tries to twist their
heads off on the table's edge
the way Cyril tells him to. but
some of these fish having
necks thick as a wrist, Ross
struggles and Cyril shows him again
using his weight, using the table's
edge, until he gets it down pat.

taking the fish last, Cyril
moves his knife twice, down
one side of the spine and back with
a quick jerk, stripping the spine away
like a chain of ice,
his blade never touching the meat,
laid flat now, the white
triangular ware, the Newfoundland trade,
and he skids that into a barrel
for Pete to scrub.

the table's old wood gets
plush with blood then ridged
in grey scum and Pete sloshes
a bucket of water under our hands

and the scuppers gradually clog and we
move knee-deep in fish and blood
a thick pool washing heads and entrails
under us and blood drips from our jackets
spatters our faces and dries and
spatters our faces again, and I squeeze
my gloved hands and the fat and blood
pour out of them like gravy
and all around the air is flashing
white gulls, shrill with their crazy
hunger, wheeling, diving to
fight for the floating guts.

all this life being
hacked apart, us letting
blood out of its envelopes,
the world suddenly seems to be all
alive, blood running inside
of us and outside of us, inside
our hands and over them, with little
between the two, a cover of skin
keeping me in or out I'm not
sure which, but some sharp
bones have gone into my hands
and some of the running blood is mine.

• clear day
island summit under my feet. sea spreads
curves up all round turning to
space: blue
field of the sun.

most ancient
most simple sight.
I stand on the first letter of earth's alphabet.
tower of stone and air.
nothing behind this bull's eye of power.
nothing higher.

eagle god.
wind's first eyes.

the green lands drift
at my feet.

●

I go back to Jewelleen. I tell her we're getting married. She's drunk. A prim wobbly smile wandering over her face. Cigarette ash down her pink v-neck. She doesn't say no. I'm there, that's all. I'm what's happening now, the direction the world has taken. She stumbles and giggles, and so do I. Arm in arm we fall, once in a tavern, once in the road, many times at the boarding house. We swim over the floor, up and down the stairs, tangled in curtains and blankets. Lying down's like holding the world to your cheek.

Her whole family stumbles and flounders with us. Uncles and cousins in every room, bent double, clinging onto the furniture. 'Brog snoll wog jeeze-a-wack,' I say to a dark scrawny man. 'Mizes-moses. Mizes-moses,' he growls with spittled fervour, gazing into my eyes, clutching my arm.

With two of us in it her bed sags more and more. We lie in a clump. A slowly squirming knot like jigged squid. The bed, her body, my whole past, the whole dark world: a dream I contend with: hills, various faces milling, rising falling. Her skin has the taste of onions and powdered rock. Her tongue tastes of bacon. Woodsmoke. Sour milk.

All night her brothers have worked hard stripping my car. Squinting over their cigarettes, muttering rapidly, they hand parts of the engine back and forth over the breakfast table, showing me where they were wearing out. They like me. I'm part of the family now. I notice one of them's wearing my shirt.

At the wedding we dance in a big dark room. A country and western band and everyone stands back in a circle while Jewelleen and I start it off. We hug and shuffle and spin around a bit and then the weight's off our feet and it's much easier and I know we've fallen down. Everyone else soon doing the same. The room going round and round. Dark shapes. A herd of seals under the red and blue bulbs.

They slap my back a lot, these toothless wiry men. They see

I don't stand on ceremony, that I've got no delicate plans for myself, that I've given my body not only to Jewelleen but to all of them, to the whole place, the way they have done. That's their *thing* - and we understand one another - drunk, the music blaring, sweating in ancient suits, brothers in sacrifice.

They've thrown their bodies away in advance of death. It's what a man does. Not only for work, burning themselves up for the young, for the women. But for death itself. For the bay and the hills holding all of the dead. For the songs. For being a man.

And I dance with all the old women and pinch them, and they laugh and pinch me back.

•

I'm thinking now about next year, about fixing this place up. Should write to Carm and see if he'd mind. Maybe he'd sell me the place, though Cyril tells me to do what I want, that Carm's beyond all that and won't ever be back. And if everything worked out I could bring some paint and window glass and tools, and fix Carm's old boat too, learn how to do that, and bring Peter and Anna and Karen here. Offer this power to them if I can.

- Haven't seen the Wellons now for four days. Which is strange, since I don't think they've taken their cod traps up.

- Used to seeing myself as a child here, knowing so much less than everyone else, so soft and helpless by comparison, it hits me all of a sudden I'm older than them. I'm like one of the ancestors they revere. Like their great-great-great-grandparents I'm just discovering the place, just figuring it out. Which makes me less of a child in a way. More of a patriarch.

• I use Carm's brook only for fresh water now, having learned to fish straight from the sea. I find the sea-run trout always thick off the point for some reason and eager to take the lure. The water I get for drinking is clear brown, nearly as dark as tea, and it tastes of the island, the rock and peat, years underground.

• warm sounds: the gas lamp's
loud hiss

the stove snaps and flutters

outside
the wind
the cold wash of gravel and sea

• A strange shaking comes over me here at the end, knowing the end is near. Frost on the grass this morning, the sky's sharp blue soaked into everything, and I know going south I'll be going back in time, back into warmer days and I need that now, trembling at how I'll change being with Karen again, back into flesh and blood, time thickening, slowing me down, letting me out of the spear point narrowing line this place is paring me to.

• a small crack first in the morning's
spell. the tall clarity, wind and sea
and birds' talk thinly mixing, holding
everything in a blue shell, and then?
a speck. a gust. crows' clatter far
at the edge? some faint hammering
some coarse-toothed saw making a hole,
a sound I recognize, and I'm out of
the cabin the end of land at my feet
and low in the blue curve beyond the
last shimmering line, eastern light
is catching a boat's white face and
I'm shaking now knowing the slow
gravelly beat with Nels at its centre
staring into the sun, and I'm
inside throwing things into a bag,
home, Karen, my children, their
faces their bodies and running once
more to the brook the blunt speech
of peat my feet do not move, my arms
have gone over my head, waving as Nels
ploughs closer down the blue hill

A Note on the Text

Many people helped me in writing this book. I thank especially Russell Brown, Don Coles, Dennis Lee, Jennifer Glossop, Al Pittman, and Adrian Fowler for their advice and encouragement; also, for help in gathering information and ideas, Wally Skinner, Earl Pilgrim, the late Ches Cassell, the Cassell brothers, George Story, George Casey, Michael Staveley, Scott Jamieson, and Anne Thareau; and for their friendship and hospitality on another island: Jane Rabnett, Klaus and Marlene Pfeiffer, and David Chater.

I am grateful to the Canada Council, the Newfoundland Arts Council, and Sir Wilfred Grenfell College, Memorial University of Newfoundland, for their support.

Parts of *The Grey Islands* first appeared in *Queen's Quarterly, Descant, The Fiddlehead, Cross-Canada Writers' Quarterly, Poetry Canada Review,* and *The Newfoundland Quarterly.* My thanks to the editors of these magazines.

About the Author

John Steffler was born in Ontario in 1947, but since 1975 has lived in Corner Brook, Newfoundland, where he teaches at Sir Wilfred Grenfell College. His other books of poetry are *An Explanation of Yellow* (1981), *The Wreckage of Play* (1988), and *That Night We Were Ravenous* (1998). He has also written a children's book, *Flights of Magic* (1987), and a novel, *The Afterlife of George Cartwright*, which won the Smithbooks/Books in Canada first novel award and the Thomas Raddall Award. It was shortlisted for the Governor General's Award and the Commonwealth Prize for Best First Book.